T0154122

In It for the Long Haul

IN IT FOR THE
LONG
HAUL

*Overcoming Burnout & Passion Fatigue
as Social Justice Change Agents*

KATHY OBEAR

NEW YORK

LONDON • NASHVILLE • MELBOURNE • VANCOUVER

IN IT FOR THE LONG HAUL
Overcoming Burnout & Passion Fatigue
as Social Justice Change Agents

© 2018 Kathy Obear

Published in New York, New York, by Morgan James Publishing in partnership with Difference Press. Morgan James is a trademark of Morgan James, LLC. www.MorganJamesPublishing.com

The Morgan James Speakers Group can bring authors to your live event. For more information or to book an event visit The Morgan James Speakers Group at www.TheMorganJamesSpeakersGroup.com.

ISBN 9781683508175 paperback
ISBN 9781683508182 eBook
Library of Congress Control Number: 2017916262

Front Cover Designer:
Rachel Lopez
www.r2cdesign.com

Interior Design:
Christopher Kirk

In an effort to support local communities, raise awareness and funds, Morgan James Publishing donates a percentage of all book sales for the life of each book to Habitat for Humanity Peninsula and Greater Williamsburg.

Get involved today! Visit
www.MorganJamesBuilds.com

Advance Praise

I felt deeply moved reading this book. As someone whose life work is committed to racial justice, I felt seen and understood. I also felt relieved, because Kathy goes beyond affirming that social justice work in this profoundly disturbing political climate is challenging; she offers the sustenance and focus needed for continuing. Now more than ever we cannot set this burden down, and Kathy offers a way to stay true to our convictions while also nurturing ourselves so that we might be as effective as possible. This isn't about giving up or even taking a break—it's about how to fight for justice from a position of internal strength. In the words of Mary Church Terrell, in her latest book, Kathy Obear yet again lifts as she climbs."

- Robin DiAngelo, PH.D., Author of *White Fragility*

"Honest, insightful, challenging, and hopeful. That is what I feel after reading the latest inspiring work of Dr. Kathy Obear. For years, I have found her work to reach millions where no one else can, in the heart. For all who are feeling the stress and strain of social justice work, this is a must read, because giving up is not an option and Kathy won't let you, instead she will inspire you."

- Eddie Moore, PH.D., Director/Founder, The Privilege Institute

"Thank you Kathy Obear! Your insights and tools have breathed fresh life into me when I needed it most. Especially powerful is the understanding that when we all focus on our unique roles in the movement, and not try to be all things to all people, we not only sustain ourselves, we create a more vibrant and resilient movement. Humanity meets strategy. Brilliant!"

- Debby Irving, Author of *Waking Up White*

"Unfortunately, many of us can relate to burnout and passion fatigue. Fortunately, Kathy Obear has written a book that can really help! Filled with useful tools for self-reflection and restoring balance, In it for the Long Haul offers a vision and strategies for being more effective social justice activists without sacrificing our well-being."

- Diane Goodman, ED.D., Author of *Promoting Diversity and Social Justice: Educating People from Privileged Groups*

"Another insightful resource from Kathy Obear that assists change agents searching for tools to get 'unstuck' and stay rejuvenated and focused in their journey toward making a difference in the world. Kathy's reflections and personal journey serves as a model for how sustainable change can happen while we also have a joyful balanced life. This book helped me imagine what this world could look like if I brought as much vigilance to living with love and compassion for myself as I do justice work."

- Lisa Landreman, PH.D., editor of *The Art of Effective Facilitation: Reflections from Social Justice Educators*

Obear's insights about the factors contributing to burnout and strategies for incorporating effective self-care to prevent it are especially needed by social justice educators working to address the unprecedented challenges facing society following the election of 2016. This book is a must read for anyone who wants to lead a healthier life while creating transformative change in our world.

- Nancy, Evans, PH.D., Author of *Disability in Higher Education: A Social Justice Approach*

"Dr. Obear provides the necessary tools to 'stay in it' as she shares her own journey. Thank you for your insights and reminders of being true to ourselves in our passion to create change."

- becky martinez, ed.d., Infinity Martinez Consulting

"At the core of social change must be the beat of sustainable people. To make meaningful social change for the long haul as change agents, we must take care of our whole selves, psyche, spirit and body and we must not let the care of self be sidelined until after the world is changed. This inspiring book does more than merely restore and underscore the agency of change makers, it is a soulful map for how to avoid burnout and passion fatigue to make meaningful social change for the long haul."

- Beth Applegate, Co-author of *Embracing Cultural Competency in the nonprofit sector: A capacity builder's guide*

"Teaching about oppression and social justice is never easy for both students and teachers. In It For The Long Haul: Overcoming Burnout and Passion Fatigue as Social Justice Change Agents speaks to me on how to deal honestly with my anxieties, assumptions and emotional responses in the teaching of anti-oppressive education. A valuable resource for everyone."

- Dennis Francis, PH.D., author of *Troubling the Teaching and Learning of Gender and Sexuality Diversity in South African Education*

"Kathy Obear really gets what it means to run in the marathon of social change. She also gets how easy it is for this work to burn us out and how crucial it is that we not let that happen. Her supportive approach combines body, mind, spirit, and heart: the thoughts, feelings, and actions we can choose to keep us going. She's skillful at coaching folks to shift our approach—things we can control—in ways that sustain us. And when we sustain ourselves, we can sustain the movement."

- Kat Morgan, ChangeAbility Solutions

Also by Kathy Obear

But I'm NOT Racist:
Tools for Well-Meaning Whites

Turn The Tide:
Rise Above Toxic, Difficult Situations in the Workplace

Dedication

For all the social justice change agents who have come before. I am deeply grateful, deeply humbled by your leadership, passion, persistence, and sacrifice so we may live in greater freedom and liberation.

To all those who have picked up the mantle to move us onward, thank you.

Together we can and together we will.

Table of Contents

Introduction

I woke up on November 9, 2016 in a deeper despair than I could remember. I wondered if anything I'd been doing really mattered. The work of so many, their sacrifices for decades, for centuries, all seemed to be wiped out in an instant. Despite evidence of horrific police brutality toward black and Latino people over the past several years, I still believed we were making progress. Now, after the national election, things seemed so much worse. Where before, it seemed we were beginning to create greater access, equity, and justice for more people in the country, suddenly it seemed all we had worked for was being dismantled and destroyed. The rolling back of our progress intensified day after day. I felt so powerless, hopeless, and depressed.

I found I wasn't alone and many people were feeling like I was. So many were already feeling close to burnout from these recent years of protests and resistance and previous years of working for systemic change. The election results felt like a punch in the gut and all the wind was knocked out of us. Yet, we kept going. In our own ways, we stepped up, we marched, we organized, we held forums, and pushed even harder knowing the stakes were increasingly dangerous and deadly for most everyone we knew and so many we may never know.

Today, I am meeting more and more people who are very close to deep burnout. In my workshops and coaching sessions, so many of us are running on empty. We sleep just enough to have the energy to pull ourselves out of bed and go back to work. We dream about the day we finally get to sleep in just an extra hour, maybe take a half-day off, or get to binge on Netflix.

One of my clients, Chris, told me:

"What more do they want from me? I am doing all I can! I am so exhausted I can hardly get out of bed in the morning. I have nothing left to give. I feel like I am drowning. But there is so much work to be done! I have to finish the Diversity Strategic Plan for the divisional meeting next week and write my remarks for the Social Justice Conference this weekend. And I have to show up at the protest later today and show my support. And I don't know when I will find time to call the legislators before Friday's vote. Plus, the budget is due next Thursday. It will be a long weekend of work.

And Jules and the kids will be frustrated again. I know I promised to go to their soccer games on Saturday. Maybe if I stay late all week, I can find time to go. I am just so overwhelmed with how much I have to do and how many people keep calling me and my office for help and support. I can't do it all! Even with all we are doing, some days, I wonder if any of this ever makes a difference? I have these nagging thoughts most every day: Am I doing what

I'm supposed to be doing? Is there something more? I used to find such joy in my early days of activism. I had such energy, so much passion. Yet, every time I move up in the organization, I feel farther away from what I love to do. All the administrative work, all the politics are so draining. I know what I do is important, but some days I feel like a sell-out, like I am colluding to make more money, to live an easier life.

I don't know how much longer I can keep this up and I am scared to death that I will just burnout and drop out all-together. Who would I be if I'm not an activist, a change agent? What would my friends think of me? Would they still be a part of my community? How can I look myself in the mirror if I slow down and do less social justice change work? But if I don't do something different, and soon, I don't know what will happen....

Things have gotten so much worse and there are so few of us really trying to change things in the organization. Fewer people are coming to our community planning meetings, especially after the blow-up we had last month. Even now, the meetings are so tense and full of arguments and disagreements. I know it can't be all fun, but this is getting so tiresome. How can we help create change if we can't even work out our own issues as a group?

And Jules had another talk with me last night. She is so mad at me these days and keeps pressuring me to do less, be home more, be more fun and playful. More time for just us. I am trying my best, but when I get a call about another crisis, she knows I have to drop everything and get on the phone. Some things can't wait. People count on me and there would be serious consequences if I don't show up and take care of things. I am barely holding it together. Trying to keep her happy, the kids happy, my boss happy, my team happy. When do I get to be happy? I don't even know what that means anymore."

This is how many of my clients are feeling these days. They are working longer and longer hours, spending less time at home, and feeling exhausted much of the time. What they want to feel is the deep passion and boundless energy they used to have so they have the stamina to create significant, meaningful change in the world and in their organization. That is exactly what this book is about. In it, I hope you find more ways to take better care of yourself so you have the capacity and resilience to stay rooted in your purpose and vision as you partner to create sustainable change.

Unfortunately, there are tens of thousands, if not millions, of change agents who are feeling the early to late stages of burnout and what I call Passion Fatigue. For me, passion fatigue is when we are going through the motions, but we have lost our spark and source of energy to keep going. It is when we want to be committed for the long haul, but have trouble believing we can make it some days. We believe in a vision of what is possible, but lately, we feel so depleted and discouraged that we question what it is all for. We have trouble finding, much less sustaining our passion, energy, and spirit as a social justice change agent. We still believe everyone deserves equity and justice, good housing and health care, liberation from oppression, and access and opportunity to lead fulfilling, meaningful lives. But some days, we can't imagine it is remotely possible. We lose our hope, we lose our passion, we lose our direction, and we lose ourselves in the process.

Yet we feel guilty and ashamed for wanting to take a break, so we push ourselves even harder to make a difference. As a result, we end up more exhausted, more easily triggered, and feeling increasingly overwhelmed by the seemingly endless waves of hurt, pain, fear, and injustice. We keep going, running on empty, until we collapse.

There is another way. It is possible to live a full, joyful life and sustain our deep passion and commitment to social justice. In fact, we may significantly increase our impact and usefulness in the world if we intentionally lead a balanced, less stressed life.

"There are a lot of people out there who are struggling. But I can't lift someone else up if I don't take care of myself, too."

~ Laverne Cox

I wrote this book for change agents who are questioning how they can be of service, how they can make a meaningful difference when they are already feeling so depleted and burned out. I wrote this book in hopes that others will find the depths of inspiration and passion they need to keep going as we all strive to elevate our efforts and leave the legacy of liberation and healing we envision is possible.

I am not sure I would have picked up this book in my early years of activism. I was so externally focused and so driven to keep going. I saw needing to take a break as a sign of weakness and low commitment to the cause. So, I kept going and pushing myself, never realizing that every time I got sick and was flat out on my bed for 7-10 days, I was of little use to anyone. Then I would feel a little better and throw myself back into my work full force until I got sick again a few weeks later. I ran this never-ending cycle for years, believing I was making a difference. All of my frantic activity and busy-ness gave me the comforting illusion of usefulness. Today, I know I could have been a far greater instrument of change if I had been more spiritually grounded, emotionally present, and physically healthy.

There are many ways to read this book. You may want to start from the beginning and read straight through as you connect with the examples and complete the recommended activities. Or you may find it more useful to jump ahead to particular chapters that speak to you, such as Chapters 2 and 3 to explore the signs and symptoms of burnout and passion fatigue, Chapter 4 if you want some talking points and strategies to persuade leaders to prioritize self-care in your organization, or Chapters 5 and 6 to identify specific self-care and community care tools and strategies to get some relief now. However you choose to read this book, I believe it can help you find more tools to diminish burnout and rekindle your passion to manifest the world you envision. Sometimes I wonder if I had read this book when I was younger, would I have been a far more effective change agent then and now? I might have developed greater capacity to avoid burnout and debilitating stress years ago. I hope you give yourself the gift of time and focus to immerse yourself in this book. I guarantee people in your lives will notice the difference and be grateful you invested in yourself in this way. I believe, in a short time, you will notice the difference as well.

I hope some of the stories, tools, and lessons learned support you through these times of deep stress and struggle. In writing this book, I pulled from my decades of experience working with and supporting change agents who are strategizing to create greater social justice within organizations, as well as from the reflections of participants in a survey I conducted this spring. I also believe the tools and concepts in this book may be useful to those in social justice movements that focus on creating change from the outside.

"This work is exhausting, and in order for us to maintain the momentum we must step in for one another. I am trying to practice what I preach, but under this administration it's proving difficult to take care of our physical and emotional well-being. But we must, because this is not a sprint, it's a marathon."

~ Linda Sarsour

We will need all of us and many millions more around the world showing up as our best selves to imagine and create new, innovative strategies and solutions. We cannot afford to have a single change agent drop out due to burnout and passion fatigue. In fact, we need to find ways to exponentially expand our numbers and create productive coalitions across differences and social justice issues. We need many more collaborative, coordinated, and sustainable strategies to dismantle oppression and create true liberation for all.

There is no time to waste. The dangers and threats are increasing every day. Our lives and those of the billions around the world depend on our collective ability to create social justice now. Not in a decade, not in twenty years, but now. We need each and every one of us present, healthy, energized, and working together to create innovative approaches and solutions so we have the stamina to resist, manifest solutions, and truly create the world we envision. For this to happen, we each have to learn how to avoid burnout and passion fatigue as we muster the capacity to stay in it for the long haul.

CHAPTER 1

I Can Spot It, Cause I Got It: My Story

"The most fulfilled people are the ones who get up every morning and stand for something larger than themselves. They are the people who will care about others, extend a helping hand to someone in need or will speak up about an injustice when they see it."

~ Wilma Mankiller

At some point when I was growing up, I came to deeply believe in Wilma Mankiller's message: that I was to live in ways that helped others and created greater fairness and justice in the world. Even in my teens, I remember feeling passionate about social justice. I wrote papers in high school about civil rights and racial justice and about the travesties of the prison system. In college, I found more anger and greater passion as I learned more about the inequities and injustices throughout history and the current manifestations of colonization and oppression around the world. I wanted to make a difference with my life, I just wasn't yet sure how.

> *"We have an obligation to fight for the world*
> *as it should be."*
>
> ~ Michelle Obama

I passionately believed in fighting for the world as I believed it should be. And fight and argue I did. It has taken a long time to learn other ways to courageously engage, that, for me, have been far more productive and sustainable.

In graduate school, I caught fire to address issues of sexism and homophobia in colleges and in society. In my first jobs as a college administrator, I channeled my activism into training others about oppression and challenging them to speak up and interrupt microaggressions and discrimination. I was passionate and energized as I worked long hours, long weekends to get my job done so I had the time to invest in social justice work. I'm sure you noticed how I had these as two separate aspects of my life.

I failed to realize that over time, I was losing my passion, my fire for this work. I felt more tired and depleted, but I kept going, until I couldn't. I have experienced severe burnout multiple times in my life. I wouldn't wish that depth of exhaustion and despair on anyone. I am grateful that I somehow pulled through each time to rekindle my commitment and energy for this work. But many do not. I believe we are each responsible for modeling ways of activism that show it is possible to be a powerful change agent while at the same time sustaining our passion, commitment, and usefulness throughout our life. The ways we show up in the work may vary over time, but we can demonstrate to others how to integrate activism into our lives throughout the decades.

I came by my unhealthy, stress-filled ways of living quite naturally. The subtle messages and modeling about self-care were in the air I breathed at home, at school, and in most every interaction I had in the world. Growing up, I never realized how I absorbed these from my parents, teachers, and society in general.

As a young girl, I was immersed in the sexist socialization that pressured and shaped me to find my sense of self-esteem and self-worth from taking care of others. Through modeling and messaging, I learned very quickly that I would be appreciated, recognized, and rewarded if, and usually only if, I worked hard to anticipate and meet the needs of others, do many chores around the house and in the yard, stop what I was doing to respond to requests for help, and always put another's needs before my own.

I watched my mother work from morning until evening taking care of so many household responsibilities: parenting, shopping, chauffeuring us to doctor's appointments, paying bills, cooking, cleaning, helping with homework, reading bedtime stories, and caring for my grandmother. In addition, she often typed reports for my father's work as well. I hardly ever saw her sit down or do something to relax. If we were watching TV as a family, she was often ironing, writing checks, or knitting afghans for each of us kids.

My father seemed to be constantly working as well. He was an independent consultant as an engineer and left early each morning for different meetings and jobs, came home for dinner, and then spread out his plans and blueprints on the dining room table to work into the night. I have fond memories of family camping vacations to Ocean City, MD when mom would slather us with sunscreen and watch over us as we played in the waves and on the beach. All the while, dad would be in the van with his plans as he worked on some project.

In elementary school, I remember having lots of freedom to play outside with friends and go on adventures in the woods behind our house. I had some chores to do but they rarely interfered with my playtime. As I got older and entered junior high and high school, I remember having more responsibilities for cleaning the house, mowing the lawn, and baby-sitting my brother. I had far less free time to do much of anything as I came home from school, started my homework before dinner, helped clean-up after eating, and then worked into the night to finish my homework before bed. Weekends were often filled with household chores as well as more homework. I did get to spend some time watching TV, socializing with friends, and often baby-sitting to earn gas money. It seemed the only time I got to rest deeply or got special attention was when I was ill. Some of my favorite memories are of weekend camping trips with the Girl Scouts, though as I look back, we were almost always working: setting up tents, collecting fire wood, digging latrines, cooking, and cleaning up. Often my favorite moments were times of rest when we sang around the campfire at night.

"When I first started my career as a social worker, I believed that my job was to change the world. That made for a daunting to-do list! I was always convinced that I could be doing more or making a bigger difference. Normally, I'm a hopeful person, but my schedule soon left me feeling exhausted and put out. I also resented anyone who wasn't as busy as I was."

~ Brené Brown

I so relate to this quote. I believed early on I was to change the world and believed that I could. I threw my whole self into my work and then played just as hard on the off-hours. I was burning my candle at both ends, and proud of it. I had no idea how costly the price would be for these life choices. I wore my busy-ness and over-working like a badge of honor. I didn't pay as much attention to the quality of my work as to how many hours and weekends I was working. I used these long hours of work to prove to others and to myself that I was worthwhile and important. My unconscious motto was "work till you drop," believing that only then was I deserving of taking time off.

I was able to keep up this schedule for some time or so I thought. I wasn't aware of how, like a bucket with a small hole at the bottom, I was leaking precious energy and life force day in and day out. I might feel better after a good night's sleep or a weekend away, but the slow, steady drip was taking its toll over time.

The irony is that early in my career I facilitated workshops on wellness, alcohol awareness, and codependency in my organization and at regional and national conferences. They say, "You teach best what you most need to learn." I could teach others how to lead balanced, healthy lives but all the while I was breaking every principle I was sharing. As I look back, I now realize I was burning out. I was increasingly irritable and resentful as I was losing compassion for others. I started to isolate more and take every opportunity to close my door and shut out the world. I was stressed out much of the time and felt unappreciated for all the extra work I was doing. I began to get behind on projects and miss deadlines. To compensate, I worked even longer hours, but this just increased my feelings of resentment. I began to judge my colleagues as less committed and less competent as I saw them lead a more balanced life than I was. Needless to say, the quality of my working relationships suffered as I got more burned out.

As I laid in bed with yet another cold or flu, I would think: "What more do they want from me? I am doing all I can!" I was so exhausted I could hardly get out of bed in the morning. I felt I had nothing left to give. I felt like I was drowning. Even as I lay there aching and in pain, all I could think about was how much work I needed to do. I made a list in my head of all the projects I needed to complete, all the programs I needed to develop. And as I looked ahead at my schedule, I felt so exhausted and depleted, but knew I had to get to work sooner than later.

Even with all I was doing, I still felt lonely. Not many people seemed to appreciate all that I did. In meetings, people seemed more distant or irritated with me. Hardly anyone acknowledged my comments or invited me to lunch or to hang out after work.

An experience during my last year as a college administrator illustrated my level of burnout and passion fatigue at that time in my life. I remember going to a committee meeting on alcohol abuse on campus. As we began to brainstorm ideas for awareness programs, I reacted in ways that were detrimental to the group's work. I was argumentative, cynical, and pessimistic. My negative energy brought the group's work to a halt. I was judgmental and critical of every idea, yet had no suggestions of my own. I felt so miserable, powerless, and ineffective. I never went back to that committee. I just disappeared without a word. While some may have been thankful I dropped out, I know I could have made a difference. If I had been my best in those meetings, I could have been an active contributor in shifting campus dynamics; and maybe I would have had a significant impact on the lives of individual students. But I was too burned out to be of any use.

I knew I needed to take a break and let my body and psyche rest, refuel, and repair. But I was afraid to stop working. Any time I slowed down or took a day off, my mind would swirl and obsess with negative thoughts, such as, "Work is piling up; I'm going to miss that deadline; I'll let people down if I don't get that done. There is so much pain in the world, I have to keep going." Under those thoughts was a deeper truth: I didn't know who I was if I wasn't working long hours. I had built my entire sense of worth and self-esteem around hard work and making a difference in people's lives. Who would I be if I slowed down?

The harder I pushed myself, the more often I fell into the all-too-familiar pendulum swing: I would work until I was exhausted, get sick, and drop out for a while. I missed work, social activities, and community events. I would stay in bed until I felt just better enough to go back to work, but not long enough to get healthy. And the pattern would repeat, over and over. I saw my frequent illnesses as evidence of my dedication and hard work. Denial is a powerful drug.

Somewhere I had heard the phrase, "Listen to the whispers, before they become screams," but I never really understood what that meant. Today, I do. As the years progressed, I kept up my pattern of over-working, exhaustion, and stopping to rest only when I got sick. It seemed normal to me. I remember having the flu and being so sick I couldn't drive myself to a training 8 hours away. During a blizzard, my partner drove me up to that university as I slept the best I could. Somehow, I was able to do the training session and get back in the car, as she drove me home to fall into bed for a week. Most any reasonable person would be shocked and deeply concerned with this story. It was just another day of work for me. This is how out of control my life was or more accurately, how out of control I was in my life.

> *"And I've learned that I always have to be on the watch for burnout. Because when it creeps up on me, I don't like the person I become. That person does not reflect my values, and she's not who I want to be..."*
>
> ~ Brené Brown

I didn't realize it at the time, but my over-working and high stress lifestyle was negatively impacting my relationship and my social life. I was traveling so often and working long days when I was home to prepare for my next consulting trip. I wasn't prioritizing time with my partner or carving out time to socialize with friends and nurture a community of support. I isolated more and more as I centered my life around work. While I may never know for sure, I also believe that the quality of my social justice work was negatively impacted as well. People may have felt I was doing good work, but today I know how much more effective and useful I can be when I am more centered and grounded in my life.

"Life will let you get away with something
for a while, but sooner or later, you will pay
the price. Everything you do in life causes the
effects that you experience. When you get the
bill, be prepared to pay."

~ Iyanla Vanzant

Then I started to have some persistent, chronic pain. Before this time in my life, I could sleep off an illness, take a lot of pain medicine, and push through. But I hadn't listened to the whispers, and the message from the universe got a little louder. Yet not loud enough for me to make any changes. I lived with a severe ache in my lower left abdomen for quite a while. I just thought this was part of growing older and working harder. Maybe I was scared to go to a doctor in case it was more serious than I thought. By then, my mom had died of cancer and my dad had committed suicide, in my opinion, out of fear that he was experiencing dementia. As the pain got more unbearable, I eventually went to a gyne-cologist and was relieved there was nothing to indicate cancer or some other significant disease. But the pain persisted. I finally got willing to try alternative medicine and found some relief through acupuncture and other forms of healing work.

I now believe that our stuck emotional energy manifests in our bodies and can lead to significant illness. I will never know what might have happened if I hadn't finally begun to take better care of myself. My fear is that I would have experienced cancer in my late

30's, and given my depleted state of health at that time, I am not sure I would have lived this long.

I was still deeply committed to making a difference in the world, but I was sick and tired of feeling exhausted and depleted all the time. My body and lack of health had gotten my attention enough that I made some major changes in my life. Over a period of several years, I got sober and stopped eating wheat, dairy, and refined sugar. With regular acupuncture and daily herbs, I slowly started to rebuild my health and immune system. But I was still getting far too many colds and flus to be able to work at the level I wanted to.

Eventually, I realized I needed to turn my focus inward and do a much deeper level of inner work and healing to clear away the stuffed emotions, resentments, fear, and deep anger that still fueled much of my life. This inner work has not always been easy. I resisted doing deep healing at times and distracted myself with work and other commitments. But I know in my soul I am a far more effective change agent when I engage others from a place of compassion, humility, and accountability. I can only stay in this place if I consistently do my inner work to show up as a clear instrument for change. I am on the path, just not at the destination yet.

There were several key milestones that helped me develop a more balanced, healthy life. Deciding to get sober, not just stop drinking, but to prioritize 12-Step programs was a significant period of healing and transformation. My next step was to change what I ate and pay much more attention to what I put into my body. Both of these made a significant difference in my energy and health. My next level of transformation occurs as I intentionally focus on doing consistent inner healing work and shift my thoughts, fears, and emotions in the moment as I navigate my triggered reactions.

I had another significant turning point in my late 50's as I gained more clarity about the types of change work I wanted to do in this next stage of my life. I became clearer about my current passions and what brought me joy as a social justice educator. I am convinced I do my best work when I am in the flow and grounded in love and compassion as I challenge others to live their lives in alignment with their core values. In this most recent process of reflection and self-renewal, I have become more selective in the types of work I do and more aware of how tightly I had been scheduling my travel, training, and coaching.

Today, I intend to have a more balanced life as I work with people and organizations that are committed to the necessary depth of change to create greater equity and inclusion for the full breadth of the people they serve. I intend to work with those who are willing to develop the capacity and courage to dismantle dynamics of oppression in themselves and in their organizations. I intend to invest my remaining years and life force in people who are truly open and committed to creating meaningful, sustainable change and transformation.

I'm not saying the work is easy, but the context and container for my trainings and coaching sessions have shifted. I leave far less exhausted and drained, often feeling refilled by the movement I see. Let me be clear, I am still learning how to manifest this new vision for my work in the world. I still occasionally accept work with an organization that I soon realize is not ready for this level of work and I quickly notice the impact this has on my self-care. I am learning how to take better care of myself in situations that are draining and challenging while I recommit to aligning my service work with those who are primed for transformative change.

I wish I could say that after several difficult periods of deep burnout over the years, I have successfully figured out how to live a balanced, sustainable life as a passionate social justice change agent. Unfortunately, I still struggle at times. My most recent wake-up call occurred as I was pushing my computer bag and pulling a carry-on through a narrow hallway on my way to the airport metal detector. I still don't know how I ended up flipping over my bag and breaking my fall with my left hand. Even though I was screaming in pain for a few moments, needing at least five minutes before I could even stand up, and couldn't move my wrist without excruciating pain, I was still standing there with the TSA agents trying to figure out how I could make the flight and show up to do a couple days of training. The only reason I finally gave in and went to the ER for treatment was I couldn't pull the bag with my injured wrist. As I was in the ambulance on the way to the hospital, I was still battling these nagging thoughts: "You could have made it; You'd made a commitment; People were counting on you; You're not that hurt." I was still plagued with self-doubt and self-recrimination until the x-rays definitively showed a broken wrist.

How often do you push yourself way past what is reasonable? How often do you cause yourself greater harm because you resist taking good care of yourself? If I'd checked my carry-on and only had my computer bag in that security line, I might have taken the flight. Who knows how much permanent damage I might have created in my wrist if I had tried to travel and train over the next two days. I know I can only be of meaningful service if I prioritize my health and self-care. But knowing wasn't enough. I still was ready to prioritize the work ahead of my critical health needs.

As I look back at that time in my life, I realize I was still overwhelmed and consumed by my despair and fear from the seemingly endless onslaught of destruction by the current administration. I was so distraught by the daily attacks on so many positive changes and so much progress that had been made over the decades. Since November 9, 2016, I had been pushing myself even harder than usual, swirling in deep emotion, and driven by my fear that I can never do enough, I will never be enough.

> *"Life sends us messages all the time and when we don't hear the message we get a lesson. If we don't learn the lesson, we get a problem. And if we don't handle the problem, we get a full-blown crisis. Get the message."*
>
> ~ Cheryl Richardson

I hope I got the message this time. I don't want to imagine how loud the next lesson may have to be for me to make enough life changes to live in balance as a change agent. Each person will need to decide and make peace with the balance between their activism, how much they contribute to creating change, and how much time and energy they invest in other areas of their lives. This is a personal decision and one that may become clearer over time.

While I generally have made peace with how I have constructed my mosaic of activism today, I still struggle and wonder if I am doing enough. I can easily start to compare myself to others who seem to be investing so much more of themselves in the work. In these moments, I try to remind myself of that 12-Step principle to avoid comparing our insides to other people's outsides. Most days I am at peace. When I'm not, I take the opportunity to look around and see how else I can be more useful, what other opportunities exist where I can share my talents and experience.

We all go through times in our lives when we are burning out and experiencing passion fatigue. The first step is to get honest and recognize how we are currently living our lives. I believe it can be useful to take a moment to reflect on our journey as social justice change agents and identify the ways we centered self-care as well as how we disregarded our own health and wellness in the process of creating change. Take a moment to look back and take stock of your life. How often have you put others first to your own detriment? Pushed yourself past exhaustion to keep showing up? Ignored the warning signs until you had to step out to recover from a serious illness? It is hard to do this level of honest reflection on our own. On my website, you can find a list of suggested prompts to guide your reflections: www.drkathyobear.com/selfcare. These may be helpful to use as you take greater responsibility to build your capacity and resilience to stay in it for the long haul.

CHAPTER 2
Why Don't We Take Care of Ourselves?

"We have just so much strength in us. If we give and give and give, we have less and less and less—and after a while, at a certain point, we are so weak and worn that we hoist up the flag of surrender. We surrender to the worst side of ourselves and then display that to others. We surrender to self-pity and to spite and to morose self-preoccupation. If you want to call it depression or burnout, well, all right...this is arduous duty, doing this kind of work; to live out one's idealism brings with it hazards."

~ Martin Luther King, Jr., From Robert Coles'
"The Call of Service: The Witness to Idealism"

I grew up with an image of activism and social justice work that involved sacrifice and a willingness to commit my whole life to a cause. As a young child, I watched when Dr. King was assassinated and later learned how many other civil rights leaders and activists were killed for trying to dismantle unjust systems and practices. In addition, the TV images of anti-war activists on college campuses and the murders at Kent State left me believing it was an all-or-nothing commitment: true activists and change agents threw their whole selves into their work, risking injury and death in the process.

And for a while, many of us can find a sense of purpose and meaning from this level of commitment. But if you are like me, and many change agents I have met, there may come a time when we have to face the reality of our life choices. The vast majority of my clients and workshop participants say they have been in dire need of self-care for a long time and are currently experiencing a deep level of burnout and passion fatigue.

What is burnout and passion fatigue?

There are many definitions of burnout, one I resonate with is: burnout is the difference between feeling tired and being bone tired. It is the difference between feeling weary and knowing you have nothing left to give.

"There are two kinds of tired, I suppose. One is a dire need for sleep, the other is a dire need for peace."

~ Sun-gazing.com

Most change agents can definitely relate to times they were so tired they needed a break to rest, refill, and refuel. These might be signs of early burnout. If we pay attention, slow down for a while and possibly take a short time out to intentionally rebuild our stores of energy and passion, we can easily re-enter our work with a renewed sense of purpose and energy. However, if we, as so many people I know, ignore these early warning signs and keep pushing ourselves to get up and show up, then we may begin to experience the signs of mid-to-late stages of burnout and passion fatigue, including deep exhaustion, hopelessness, and pessimism as well as a growing sense of apathy and despair. In the next chapter I go into far greater depth about the signs and symptoms of burnout and passion fatigue.

When we are experiencing this level of deep exhaustion, we are in dire need of a more significant shift in our lives so we can truly rejuvenate, revitalize, and realign our life choices to ensure we have the energy and capacity to work for social justice for the long haul. If we do not stop and examine our lives at this point, we will most likely experience a level of passion fatigue that may be extremely difficult from which to recover. A client shared her story of when she realized she had moved from experiencing mild burnout to passion fatigue:

"In a workshop last week, the trainer asked us to envision our future in the next 3-5 years. It was so depressing. All I could see was more of the same: working 10-12 hour days, feeling too exhausted when I got home to do much with the kids or my partner, dragging myself to community meetings and organizing sessions, and wondering what's the use anyway. I used to feel such passion and excitement as we planned marches and protests. Now, I resent having to go to another meeting just to hear the same complaints as people rage against the system but do nothing of substance to change anything. I always knew burnout was a part of social change work, but I never knew it could get this bad. I expected to feel tired and frustrated sometimes. I knew it would be hard work to keep fighting and challenging systems of oppression. I had watched some people drop out and never come back, but I just judged them as weak and more concerned about their own privilege and comfort than helping create real change in the world. And now I am afraid I have become one of them."

We invest so much of ourselves in the work. We do not compartmentalize social justice in our lives, so our life is the work. We think about and speak up about social justice in most every moment of every day. It is who we are. We raise issues to create greater liberation in our work environments and in our communities, and then, if we're parents, we are constantly focused on raising more socially aware children in a safer, more just world.

We are deeply aware of the pervasive, debilitating, and destructive impact of oppression in the daily lives of people we love and care about as well as those we may never meet. Social justice is extremely personal to us. We may feel the overwhelming severity of the pain and damage in people's lives, the ferocious strength of the resistance and obstacles to change, and the seeming apathy of the vast majority of people in our communities. As a result, many of us are fueled by a desperate sense of urgency for immediate change. This work is not a conceptual activity or an interesting discussion to us: We believe that people's lives today and those of future generations depend on the success of our work. As a result, we tend to invest all of ourselves into creating greater liberation and justice for all.

As a consequence, we are deeply susceptible to experiencing burnout. Unlike a cold or flu that many can feel coming on, burnout creeps up on us slowly and quietly. Most may not notice the gradual erosion of our energy and passion until we hit some type of personal crisis. Creating change inside organizations and in society can be not only physically demanding, but also emotionally, mentally, and spiritually draining. We are so focused on creating change, being of service, and taking care of others, we most often ignore our own needs and sacrifice ourselves for the greater good. We feel we can never disengage, never disconnect, and never let up for even a moment. As one workshop participant said, "There is no downtime, especially with this current administration. It just keeps coming. Never-ending demand, increasing demand. We can't stop now. I feel guilty just thinking about taking a couple days off." When we feel guilty even considering a small, short-term change in our lives, most of us do not take time-off, and just keep pushing ourselves, often past what is reasonable and healthy.

I ask my clients, "How much do you need self-care right now?" When they use a 0-10 scale, from not at all to completely to assess themselves, the average rating is around 8.5 with many people claiming a 10. Take a moment and ask yourself this same question. Take a few deep breaths and get quiet in your body. Do a slow scan of the physiological sensations in your body from your head to your toes. What do you notice? How would you describe your level of health and energy these days? How easy is it for you to get out of bed and feel renewed and ready to take on your day?

Now, check-in on your emotions. How are you feeling? Would you describe your emotions as more positive or negative? How intense are your different emotions? Are you feeling somewhat numb or flat? Overwhelmed or content? How much joy and happiness have you felt recently? Are you able to navigate difficult situations effectively? Can you handle mildly challenging moments or are you easily irritated and triggered these days? How often do you react less effectively, in ways you later regret or need to clean-up? How effectively are you showing up to work with others to create change? How much do you need self-care right now?

Now do a mental scan. How clear is your mind? How easily do you gather information and make decisions? How readily do you remember important information, complete key tasks, and meet deadlines? Have you been making more mistakes recently?

Now move on to scanning your spirit and level of commitment. What is your level of motivation and passion? What is your degree of hope, enthusiasm, and optimism? How does your current degree of commitment compare to a few months ago, a few years ago, or when you first started doing social justice change work?

Finally, do a scan of the quality of your relationships. What is the quality of your relationship with important people in your life: intimate partners, family members, and close friends? How would you describe your connections with colleagues at work and in other social justice groups? What is the quality of your relationship with yourself?

Take another moment to just sit with these questions and listen to your body, your heart, and your spirit. Then, get a sense of what rating best describes how much you need self-care right now using this scale:

0 = not at all

10 = completely

I encourage you to take a moment and journal about your rating, your thoughts, and feelings in this moment. Next, take a few more deep breaths and notice the level of your willingness to make the necessary life changes that could help you lower your rating. If you are like me, at times I have far more need for self-care than the willingness to change. There are so many personal, cultural, and organizational obstacles to creating a balanced life as social justice change agents. See if you relate to any of the following reasons I keep hearing from so many clients for why they do not take better care of themselves as activists and educators.

Why we don't take care of ourselves

Organizational demands

Most work environments place increasing demands on employees to do more with less. In the current climate of decreasing resources, cutbacks in staffing, and ever-increasing need, most employees are juggling a far heavier workload in a much more stressful environment. Over three decades ago, I remember counting up my weekly meetings and was shocked to see I was spending 28 hours in scheduled meetings, not counting all the informal conversations that distracted me from working on projects and creative problem-solving. Today, my guess is many people have even less flexibility in their schedules as they work evenings and weekends to try to keep up with the onslaught of emails, deadlines, and unexpected crises.

Many people I talk to complain about having too many demands competing for their time and attention, initiative overload, and ever-shifting priorities. Employees are expected to power through their workloads and produce results on timelines they rarely helped create. As one client described these dynamics, "Even if I have time to make a plan, it will soon get up-ended. They keep piling on more without prioritizing or evaluating what can be let go." In addition, many people are watching colleagues resign or get fired, without having those positions refilled. They are experiencing far less staff support as they are still expected to meet very high, unrealistic expectations from supervisors and managers. A participant talked about the impact of this "get it done now" culture, "Everything is urgent and needs to be done immediately. Or at least I think it does. And taking care of myself never gets very high on my to-do list. I worry that if I take a break, the work will continue to pile up and be impossible to dig out from under. It is easier to just keep going."

Prevailing cultural messages

In their article, *White Supremacy Culture,* Kenneth Jones and Tema Okun talk about many of the pervasive white cultural norms and practices in most U.S. organizations that undermine productivity and staff morale (Jones & Okun, 2001). http://www.cws workshop.org/PARC_site_B/dr-culture.html. Can you relate to working in organizations, even those with a social justice mission, where employees feel pressure to be perfect, to respond immediately to whatever is considered urgent by those with more positional power, where time is money and valued more than personal health or wellness, and those that work long hours and put in "face-time" are valued over others who may produce far better quality of work?

I believe our U.S. culture is grounded in workaholism and work addiction. Media constantly shows images that glorify and reward people who work long days and nights, choose work over family and relationships, and are addicted to work, power, and success. Success means working hard, doing more with less, achieving goal after goal, increasing profits, and making huge amounts of money. In these organizational cultures, self-care is considered unproductive and selfish.

Many people and organizations glorify busy-ness. Exhaustion is worn like a status symbol with people comparing how many late nights and weekends they work. If you are like me, you may buy-into these cultural messages to the point where you define your own worth and worthiness by how much you work. We use our long hours as a benchmark to prove our usefulness to others and to ourselves.

Mixed messages from organizational leaders

A client shared about the types of mixed messages she gets from her supervisor and the organization: "I am getting emails from Human Resources with tips and resources to create better work/life balance and my supervisor encourages me to take time off to manage my stress better. Yet, the work expectations far exceed my capacity to complete them in a 50-hour work week. And just now, I got two more emails about urgent meetings I need to rearrange my schedule to attend. Then when I do ask for time-off, my supervisor gets irritable, even hostile, and often denies my requests." Mixed messages are commonplace as organizations try to present an image of valuing their personnel so they can compete for top talent and increase the retention of their workforce. In reality, the culture of busy-ness and the increasing pressure for results undermines any support for self-care and wellness.

I should be able to do it all

I remember growing up with the pervasive cultural messages for women that we can, and should, be able to do it all. There was a commercial jingle that still rings in my head about the need for wives to bring home the bacon, fry it up in a pan, and still take care of your man. How many more common cultural messages perpetuated the lie and illusion that we all, especially women, can and should be able to do everything? How many messages like this still perpetuate exhaustion and burnout as well as sexism, heterosexism, classism, racism, ableism and other forms of oppression?

The sky is falling

A participant shared a very common theme I hear, "I feel like I always have to be 'on' all the time. In some social justice circles, losing time to self-care can cost lives. This is high stakes work. There is so much horror and urgency in the world. There is no time for self-care." For so many of us in roles where we serve and support others, we may never feel we can slow down or take a break. So many people I meet in workshops feel so passionate about creating inclusive organizations and are deeply pained by the daily, constant microaggressions and forms of institutionalized oppression that so negatively impact people they care about and serve.

In a workshop, one participant's comment impacted most of us in the room. They described how they were barely holding it together as they were working 24/7 to try to help the college students who were so devastated by the racism they experienced from both professors and students in classrooms as well as from people they lived with in the residence halls. The participant expressed that every student that dropped out due to the racist climate takes a huge emotional toll on them. Another participant added, "This work is very personal to me. As a woman of color and as an immigrant, these last several months have been so extremely challenging that I do not have time to take a break." Many people in the workshop agreed that the work is far more important than their self-care needs. But if we don't also keep our focus on our self-care, we won't have the energy or passion to respond in these challenging times.

Guilt

A very common reason I hear from clients for why we don't take good care of ourselves is we feel guilty when we do. We compare ourselves to other people who appear to give their whole lives to create social justice. When we come up short, we believe we don't do enough so we work even harder. As one workshop participant put it, "There is so much pain and anger, terror and hate in the world. If I don't do all that I can, I feel like I am allowing the pain and hate to grow." But what she doesn't realize is how we are far more effective as change agents if we also invest some time and energy in taking care of ourselves in the process.

Self-care is selfish, a luxury of the privileged

A participant recently expressed what I hear from so many white change agents who feel guilty for taking any time for self-care, "Since the presidential election and especially since the change in leadership, I have been obsessing about all of the hate and horror that is unleashed each and every day. I feel if I don't stay on top of it, I won't be able to do anything about it. So, I was obsessive about watching the news, getting updates on Twitter and Facebook. I felt that every update I missed was proof I wasn't a good activist, that I was politically lazy and using my privilege to sit on the sidelines."

There is a very strong message in many social justice circles that self-care is selfish and a luxury only afforded to the privileged. Another white participant talked about this same dilemma: "I feel guilty focusing on self-care when I have so much privilege I can retreat into. I work with so many who have far less ability to take time off. They keep going, working hard, doing activist change work without a break, so I can't either." The belief is we have to work as hard, if not harder, as those whose lives are on the line.

Many change agents recognize how the daily realities of life for people of color are so glaringly different from most whites. A participant of color powerfully described these dynamics, "Brown people never get down time in public. We have to smile and pretend we have patience and compassion even in the face of overt aggression, or we will be labeled as difficult, too angry, a trouble-maker. This is deeply exhausting. After interrupting and experiencing so much oppression every single day, we then go home and try to support our family who have also been targets of oppression. We try to keep them safe from getting profiled, afraid they could be killed if we let them out of our sight."

Change agents with other privileged identities may also struggle with similar types of guilt and shame for wanting to stop out for a while. The external and internal pressures to keep going no matter the consequence leave many people feeling they don't deserve self-care. As another participant put it, "I'm white and have a Master's degree. I can't take time-off to take care of myself. I don't deserve a break when people of color can't take a break from racism and people from low-income backgrounds never get relief from classism. I get so much privilege, I have to keep working to create racial and class justice."

I don't have time

The belief "I don't have time" is the most frequent reason I hear from clients and workshop participants for not focusing on self-care. I was particularly impacted hearing the stories of change agents with family responsibilities describe how they try to manage it all. One client shared how it seemed like she was walking a very thin tightrope trying to juggle everything in her life:

"I am stretched so thin these days. I am running at high speed and still can't keep up with it all. After work, I have to take care of the kids, help them do homework, cook dinner, clean the house, and try to find time to pay bills and shop for their school needs. My parents need me more now that they are aging. I take them to doctor's appointments and get their prescriptions refilled and make sure they spend time with the kids when I can swing it. I don't know what I'll do if they ever need more constant care from me. Last week the baby got sick and now I am feeling like she passed it on to me. My boss will be so pissed if I am out any more this month. I have had high stress times before, but they have come and gone. I don't see this changing any time soon. There is just too much going on, too many demands for me to pause and take care of me. And I'm gone from home doing community work so much, I feel guilty if I don't spend every bit of spare time with my family."

It can seem impossible to imagine how we can begin to take care of ourselves when we feel pulled in so many different directions. In my experience, however, the more I focus on my well-being, the greater energy, passion, and capacity I have to support others in my life.

Put life masks on others first

Contrary to the direction from flight attendants to put on our own life masks before we help others, so many activists and change agents feel compelled to put the needs of others first. We put our self-care and personal needs on the back burner and, sometimes, even those of our family. As one participant put it, "I always put other's needs before mine. And when there is a crisis at work or in the community, that takes priority over my family. I feel so guilty leaving them, but what choice do I have?"

Fear of speaking up

Many employees describe how challenging it is to focus on self-care when they work in toxic organizational climates where they battle difficult personnel issues, incompetent managers and leaders, and the constant unproductive chaos that has become normal in many organizations. They often work in a climate of fear and tension and worry about the consequences of trying to even talk about stress and self-care. As one participant said, "I'm afraid if I try to take better care for myself and speak up about my need for a more balanced life, it will hurt my reputation or may be a career-impacting move. I feel this constant need to perform and to produce. How can I ever admit I need help or ask for some time for self-care?"

While people at most levels of an organization can feel this fear of speaking up, those who work in lower-level positions may face even more pressure and punishment for raising concerns, challenging organizational norms, and taking too much sick-time, even though they have earned it. As one client said, "I just keep my head down and push through instead of raising issues with my supervisor about the unrealistic work expectations. I am afraid of advocating for myself and my team for fear we will argue and she will think less of me."

I relate to many other fears that change agents describe that result in our not speaking up, including: What will people think of me if I slow down? People will be so disappointed in me; What if I let them down? What if they think I am weak and can't handle things?

If we don't change...

At times, these cultural messages and reasons we don't focus on our self-care feel overwhelming and inescapable. Yet, when we relentlessly drive ourselves to deep exhaustion, despair, and passion fatigue, we may inevitably create what we fear most: we burn out, drop out, and lose our identity as social justice change agents. Some people get sick, engage in self-destructive behaviors, destroy relationships, and even die from the effects of not taking care of themselves.

There is another way. It is possible to help create meaningful change as well as live a balanced, joyful life. It is possible to sustain our passion, energy, and commitment to social justice for the long haul. But we first must develop deeper capacity to recognize our warning signs of burnout and make a commitment to ourselves, our families, and our social justice communities that we will be as vigilant in our own self-care as we are in creating organizational and societal change. If you weren't so exhausted and burned out, what more of an amazing difference could you make in the world? Can you even imagine?

CHAPTER 3
Warning Signs

A workshop participant spoke for me and so many other change agents on the verge of serious burnout when she shared:

"I woke up and, for a split-second, I felt really good. And then I remembered all that I still needed to get done, how far behind I was on some critical projects, and how many horrendous, oppressive actions had come out of the White House administration just yesterday. And whatever energy and optimism I had in that quick moment between waking and remembering, was long gone. I forced myself out of bed, wanting to lie there under the covers, hoping for a moment of peace. I got up, fed the cats, got dressed, and put on my shield to be able to go to work, and do it all over again."

Can you relate? How often do you have to force yourself to get out of bed or go to a planning meeting or attend a rally? We get up, we keep going, and rarely notice how our energy reserves and passion are draining away day after day.

It is critical to increase our knowledge of our personal early warning signals as well as heighten our capacity to be present enough in the moment to notice the slightest indicator of depletion in our physical, emotional, mental, and spiritual selves. If we don't, we may not recognize these whispers in time to stop our slide into deep burnout and passion fatigue. One of my clearest signals I need self-care is when a client cancels a training event and, instead of worrying about the loss of work, I am excited to have the time-off! What are your key warning signs you need more self-care? Can you list fifteen to twenty of your most common ones?

Warning signs and symptoms of burnout and passion fatigue

"If you work with the homeless and find yourself one day telling them they're lazy and should just get up and get jobs, you probably need a break. If you are increasingly disenchanted with the people or the situations that you are working to change, you probably need to take a break. This is especially so if you begin to feel that no one appreciates all your blood, sweat, and tears."

~ Tavis Smiley

As you read this chapter, I encourage you to use a journal to make a list of any of the signs of burnout and passion fatigue that sound familiar in your life right now. Can you relate to Tavis Smiley's warning about times we begin to judge, shame, and resent the people experiencing oppression, the people we are working to support? We are in trouble when we start to become more immune to all the devastations we see and stop seeing the people we are serving as deserving or worthy human beings. Are you feeling more hopeless and pessimistic about the chances for real change? Or feeling deeply disappointed and critical of your colleagues in the struggle? Can you relate to feeling unappreciated and deserving of more recognition? These are just some of the signs we are somewhere in the stages of burnout and passion fatigue.

A common early warning signal is exhaustion and feeling tired all the time. You might sleep through the alarm or keep hitting the snooze button just to get a few more minutes of rest. Many change agents struggle with insomnia and poor sleep patterns. They may wake-up in the middle of the night and obsess about all they have to do. Or toss and turn all night worrying about everything on their plate. Even taking a nap does little to make a dent in their fatigue. Some even have dreams about all the stress in their lives or experience nightmares about missing an important deadline.

Speaking of dreaming, another telltale sign I need self-care is when I catch myself in an important meeting day-dreaming about my next vacation. I usually envision a sunny, beautiful island with warm water and gentle waves. Wanting to completely check-out and unplug for a long time is a good clue I may need to do just that. Other related warning signs include how often I binge on movies and TV as well as when I lose myself in social media. It is especially concerning when these ways of checking out for a while no longer give me any relief because I am so stressed out that I am unable to relax and refuel. When I can no longer easily disconnect for a while, I am on the slippery slope to burnout.

Our stress manifests in so many work-related dynamics. Are you constantly feeling overwhelmed and obsessing about deadlines? Is your work life all about putting out fires and responding to unexpected crises? Do you put your family and relationships on the back burner every time there is a work emergency? Are more and more things being framed as emergencies at work?

I remember feeling like I was just going through the motions at work. I kept my focus on getting through the next meeting, pushing through, and checking off tasks with little energy or care about the quality of my work. Work and change efforts felt like an obligation and drudgery. I was just trying to survive and get through the day. I had lost most of my creative spark and was far less productive and effective than useful. I was easily bored and restless. I felt less energized and more lethargic, often dragging my feet and not caring about deadlines. A key indicator of stress for me is having trouble finding the energy to start projects I would usually plow right through.

If I had to begin a new task, I would feel overwhelmed and not know how to begin. As a result, I would procrastinate, isolate, and not let anyone know I was struggling. I would ignore and avoid tasks and responsibilities that may have been more critical, but were less fulfilling. I would just focus on what I knew I could do well or somewhat enjoyed doing. Needless to say, I pulled a lot of long nights and weekends to catch up so I didn't miss too many deadlines. When I was focused on just trying to get by, I would lose perspective on what was important and ignore strategic goals or even my own personal development plans. Only later would I realize and come to regret all the missed and wasted opportunities.

When we work in high stress environments, our working relationships often suffer. A participant described what many change agents experience when they are burning out:

"I can't even stand myself lately. Heaven knows how others are putting up with me. I am so irritable and angry all the time. I bit off the administrative assistant's head because the copier machine wasn't working. I am so easily triggered over the smallest inconveniences. Last night at the restaurant, we had to wait ten minutes for a table and I was coming out of my skin. I yelled at the kids for making too much noise and can't seem to control my emotions any more. And I know my boss is going to confront me for blowing up in the meeting yesterday. But I am so sick and tired of the incompetence of my colleagues!"

Do you relate to feeling far more short-tempered and irritable? Perhaps you are more impatient and judgmental than usual? All these behaviors negatively impact our working relationships in the moment and can have longer-term consequences on teamwork and morale. When I can't regulate my emotional reactions, I say and do things without thinking. This behavior usually triggers others and undermines our productivity. I'm clearly not modeling effective leadership and my inappropriate behaviors result in increased tension, conflict, and stress with my co-workers.

When I am burning out, I feel more resentment and disappointment in my colleagues, especially those in their privileged identities who aren't moving as fast or caring as much as I think they should. I question their commitment and competence and am more suspicious and distrustful of their motives. In difficult situations, I tend to fight back, defend, and debate rather than engage in meaningful dialogue. And I am far more focused on being right than on what is most needed for the organization. I am insistent that I get what I want when I want it.

> *"If you see what needs to be repaired and how to repair it, then you have found a piece of the world that G-d has left for you to complete. But if you only see what is wrong and how ugly it is, then it is you yourself that needs repair."*

~ Rabbi Menachem Mendel Schneerson

A workshop participant talked about the impact of stress in her work life, "I am so much more critical and negative at work these days. I get snappy and give off cold vibes to my colleagues. I'm more grumpy and crabby, and am just not fun to be around. I'm getting into silly arguments and even I am sick of how much I am complaining lately."

If you are like me, this negativity we have for others is also turned on ourselves. I get much more self-critical. A classic sign I need self-care is I obsess about the one or two negative comments I receive as I read the evaluations from a training session. I spend far too much time and energy trying to figure out who wrote them and what I should have done differently, and just can't let it go.

Other work-related signs I need self-care involve the quality of my listening. I am often distracted and spinning in my own mind and don't listen as well. I miss the nuances and subtle messaging in conversations. One client talked about how they had trouble focusing on others, "I was so burned out after the election and my office was flooded with students and staff who needed to process and heal. I wasn't taking care of myself and so was barely able to listen to their stories, fears, and anxieties. I felt so raw with so many of my own traumas and intrapersonal roots retriggered. I never felt good enough. It required me taking a full week off for my own healing to be able to recover enough to be useful back at work." When we are full of our own emotions and unresolved issues, we have little to no capacity to effectively support anyone else.

Another sign that we need self-care occurs when we are more compulsive and far less attentive or concerned about how we are coming across to others. Can you relate to writing that snarky, sarcastic email to someone we thought deserved it? Or making impulsive, even irrational decisions before taking the time to think through the probable impact of our actions? If we are frantic and in a whirlwind to get things done, we're more likely to step on toes, say things we later regret, and make avoidable mistakes that are time-consuming to fix.

How often does someone have to remind you what they told you just a few days ago? Are you forgetting important details or commitments? A key signal of burnout is having trouble remembering decisions from recent conversations or even people's names. When we are burned out we can't think clearly and can't keep track of things as easily. Outside of work, we lose track of important events and activities in the lives of our partner, friends, and family.

In addition to the physical fatigue, we often experience deep mental fatigue. Can you relate to losing your spark and enthusiasm? Do you feel less joy at work? Are you having less fun than you used to? Are you having difficulty making decisions? We often equivocate and flounder around, unable to set a clear direction when we are overly stressed. All of these work-related warning signs of burnout can also manifest in every aspect of our personal lives as well.

Listen to your body

Most every social justice change agent I know is near burnout and passion fatigue and experiencing multiple physiological manifestations of their stress. A couple weeks ago, my left eye kept twitching. This had never happened to me before. I would rub it, keep it closed for a while, but it just kept on trying to get my attention. What is your body trying to tell you lately? Many people report having tension headaches or migraines in times of stress. Others experience dizziness or more aches and pains in their back, neck, eyes, or joints.

An old telltale sign for me is getting sick. Many people talk about getting colds and flus and not being able to get over them easily. Like me, many go back to work before they should, and just get more run down and sick again. I believe most people try to ignore and push through these physiological symptoms of stress. I encourage you to pay more attention and consider consulting with a doctor or other health professional if you experience unexpected, persistent, and/or severe symptoms. Stress can contribute to numerous chronic and deadly diseases, including diabetes, heart disease, cancer, and high blood pressure. As more research is conducted with a social justice lens, I believe we will have even more undeniable evidence of the direct connection between oppression, marginalization, and significant health problems. We need all of us healthy and alive so we can dismantle oppression and create liberation for all.

Emotional signs of stress

A large number of my clients and workshop participants feel much more anxious and depressed when they are deeply stressed.

They describe how they feel greater sadness and cry more easily during these periods in their lives. A few clients talked about how their obsessive compulsive disorder (OCD) gets worse or they experience panic attacks and heart palpitations. One training participant pointed out the serious impact of stress on their mental health, "When I am deeply stressed, I have a far greater risk for relapsing into depression and anxiety. I have been treated clinically in the past, and it is a slippery slope." Several others described having far more feelings of worthlessness, helplessness, and powerlessness, questioning the usefulness of what they are doing. A related dynamic was described by a participant in a workshop, "I more easily slip into self-pity, woe is me. I only focus on what is hard in my life and lose perspective in my self-centeredness."

Emotional binging

A clear sign of burnout for me and so many others is emotional binging. Our relationship to food can be an immediate source of feedback on our self-care needs. Do you relate to over-eating and binging on junk food or sugary sweets when you are stressed? Maybe rationalizing these choices with the thought, "I am working so hard, I deserve to splurge." Are you gaining weight, feeling sluggish, and then beating yourself up in the process?

We can use many other substances in ways that may not be healthy for us. Brooke Castillo, Founder of The Life Coach School, calls this buffering. In addition to food, I have over-used caffeine and alcohol to try to shift my emotions or stuff my feelings. It's not just what we put in our bodies. We can emotionally binge on shopping, sex, exercise, Facebook, Netflix, sleeping—all as ways to get out of our bodies, numb out and get away from it all, if only for just a while. In moderation, most of us can enjoy these activities and they may add value to our lives. Knowing our limit and when we cross the line to binging, obsession, and addictive behavior is critical to our self-care.

Under-doing

Another warning sign for many change agents is when we stop doing activities that bring us joy and are healthy for us. When I stop exercising regularly, it is a sign my life balance is off. Do you cut back on date nights or family time to work longer hours or attend a few more community meetings? Are you living in more clutter and avoiding household chores? Did you get an over-due notice because you forgot to pay the bills? All of these could be signs you are slipping into burnout and passion fatigue.

Have you lost interest in activities you used to really enjoy? Socializing with friends? Going out to movies or dancing? Playing make-believe with the kids? Sitting for a moment having coffee with your partner? Going to a protest? Do you find yourself isolating more? Wanting to disengage, withdraw from activities that used to re-energize you?

A participant described how many of these warning signs impact the others:

"For me, so many of these signs and symptoms I need more self-care influence and aggravate each other. When I don't eat well, I feel more sluggish and often don't sleep as well. Then I am more tired and want more caffeine and junk food to give me the needed jolt to get things done. When I am not exercising consistently, I feel more stress in my body, which results in more aches, pains, and stiffness. Being in pain affects my energy and my attitude, which probably impacts others I work with."

When we choose the courage to begin to look closely, to wake up to the reality of stress, burnout, and passion fatigue in our lives, we may begin to see a complex, intersecting web of areas needing our attention.

How's your list?

Take a moment and look back over your list. Anything missing? Take a few deeps breaths and notice how you are feeling as you review the list of your current warning signals. Which ones, if any, are concerning you at this moment? Which signs are concerning to people who care about you? Who work with you? Who organize and protest with you?

"I think self-care is something deliberate, something that I do to take care of myself in a world that tells me I shouldn't necessarily exist. That my body and my identity don't necessarily matter - especially in systems that weren't built for me to really thrive. We can say that the ways in which we survive are ways in which we take care of ourselves - but I don't really think that's care- that's us trying to survive in systems that weren't built for us."

~ Janet Mock

I am grateful to Janet Mock and so many other past and current change agents who are clear about the critical role self-care plays in our capacity to be effective as we partner across differences to dismantle oppression and create true liberation and justice for all. I can feel overwhelmed when I begin to recognize how many warning signals are going off in my life and how burned out I really am. It can seem like the only thing that could possibly help is a very long sabbatical. While significant time-outs may be exactly what are needed, there are many other tools and strategies to help us get back on track to a more balanced life as change agents. The sooner we notice and accept that we are needing self-care, that we're sliding closer to deep burnout and passion fatigue, the sooner we can intervene and interrupt the cycle and get back on to a more useful life path. But even if we make different choices, we may still encounter stiff resistance from others. In the next chapter I explore some of the backlash we might experience when we make a more concerted effort to focus on our self-care.

CHAPTER 4

Look Out For Backlash and Self-Sabotage

Backlash in the workplace

Supervisors

was stopped in my tracks when a client said, "The organization thinks they own me." I encourage you to take a deep breath and sit with the impact as you reread this phrase. They went on to say how the organization expects them to be accessible at all times, 24/7, including weekends. In addition, they are expected to immediately respond to any crisis or email from top leaders. Many other people I work with have shared very similar experiences. As one told me, "Crises don't wait for self-care."

When I was a manager over three decades ago, I had some control over my calendar. I could build in time-off and arrange a more flexible schedule to compensate for my late night and weekend work commitments. I am not sure many organizational change agents experience this level of support and flexibility today. As one client put it, "People think they own my time. Even when I schedule a longer lunch to go work out knowing I am staying late to finish a project, others insist on scheduling over that time like it is theirs to control." Another client shared their supervisor's comment that left them feeling tremendous pressure to be always working, even over-working: "This is work time, not self-care time," as if these are not connected; as if there should be no place for self-care at work.

Some change agents have tried to talk with their supervisors about ways to better balance their workloads and increasing demands so they do not burn out on the job. While I have heard stories of supportive leaders who encourage, if not require, their team members to live balanced lives, these examples seem to be exceptions to the rule. One participant shared how their supervisor reacted when they brought up some concerns about work/life balance: "It is not my job as your supervisor or this department to make sure you are well. That is solely your responsibility." Unfortunately, this reflects more of the norm in most organizations, I believe.

Without intentional support from leaders and colleagues, most people struggle in isolation and hide the realities of their stress and burnout. These prevailing cultural norms to work until your drop and put the needs of the organization above your own are deeply rooted in exploitive capitalistic and classist beliefs that most people, that is, the "good employees," can easily keep up with the increasing pace of work. Therefore, those who speak up and challenge the organizational and cultural norms that perpetuate acute stress and burnout are simply people who can't hack the pressure and are not suitable workers. The underlying belief is employees are expendable and replaceable, to be used and then discarded by the organization.

Many people in my workshops have shared how hard it was to push back against the extreme, constant pressure to always do more and to be more available. They are concerned that speaking up may be career-impacting in the short-term and affect their performance appraisals. Most are acutely aware that they will need positive recommendations from their supervisors and other leaders if they ever want to apply for a promotion or a position in another organization. A client once shared how they had tried unsuccessfully to negotiate a more reasonable work schedule or comp time to compensate for long hours of unpaid work. Their next comment jumped out at me, "My supervisor forces me and a colleague to work many extra unpaid hours each week. I would quit if I could find a job that is less toxic and pays for graduate school. For now, I look for ways to manage a pretty dysfunctional situation." Many leaders and supervisors, in my opinion, seem to have no clue, or maybe just don't care, about the staggering human costs their employees experience from such over-demanding, unrelenting workplace dynamics.

Employees that do speak up may experience negative consequences and backlash from their supervisors. One participant described how their supervisor regularly makes sudden requests of them that results in their having to put other pressing projects on the backburner. When she tried to talk with her supervisor about this dynamic and negotiate a different timeline after another unexpected request, her supervisor accused her of being inflexible and lacking professionalism.

Some participants in my workshops talked about feeling surprised by the backlash from their supervisors given the positive organizational stance about self-care and work/life balance. They were caught off guard by the inconsistent messaging. As one shared, "My supervisor agreed that while I was at conferences and other professional development opportunities, I only needed to check my emails at breaks so I could be fully present in the learning experiences. As I was attending this one conference, I left an auto-email to give people options to contact for emergencies. When I returned to work, my supervisor berated me publically and privately and said I was not committed to students. She called me a poor team player for not immediately responding to emails when I was off-site." Another participant in that workshop shared a similar experience of mixed messaging, "My supervisor publically advocates for self-care and even privately praised me for prioritizing my self-care. And then recently she publically criticized me in staff meetings by questioning my commitment to the team."

I wonder if a few other comments I've heard in workshops recently are more commonplace than people realize, such as: "As a single person, I am told that colleagues with partners and/or children need more time away for self-care than I do" and "My supervisor told me I am too young, too new to the field to be burned out."

I doubt most leaders are aware of the devastating impact of these types of comments and actions on productivity, morale, and loyalty to the organization. If they did, I want to believe that they would change how they support employees to deliberately create a much more balanced lifestyle.

Workplace colleagues

In addition to pressure and backlash from supervisors, many people experience negative comments and treatment from their peers. One client shared the types of under-the-breath comments they heard as they came back from working out over their lunch hour, "I barely have time to eat lunch at my desk." A workshop participant who works in a residential facility talked about how they go to bed every night around 10 p.m. in order to get enough sleep to be energized and present in their work. They have let the residential staff they supervise know not to disturb them unless it is an emergency or crisis. In meetings and in passing, they often hear resistant comments framed as jokes, such as, "If you can go to bed at 10 p.m. each night, you must not be doing your job."

Partners and Family Members

Many clients I talk to also experience resistance from their partners and family members when they try to focus more on their self-care. Some comments may be rooted in fear of economic insecurity, "It costs too much money" or "We can't afford for you to take time off. How will we pay the bills?" Others are grounded in wanting their partners to be more available for family activities, "You're hardly around anymore. You've missed so many family gatherings this year. You need to spend more time with the children, not take more time for yourself."

A common pattern occurs when we succumb to family pressures and choose to attend events, help out our family members, and drop everything to respond to another family crisis. In many cases, we once again push aside our personal needs for rest and rejuvenation. Even when we know we are putting our health at risk, we most often choose others over ourselves. As one workshop participant commented, "People say just the right thing that pushes my guilt button and I do it so I won't feel as guilty."

Friends in Community Organizations

Some people I work with have described how they tried to cut back the amount of community change work they organized or attended in order to create a bit more ease and flexibility in their schedules. As one client said, "Sometimes I feel guilty, but I have to pull back somewhere. Last week after I had missed a couple planning meetings, one of my friends was frustrated that I hadn't attended the Board meeting and had missed the recent protest. He said I had let them down. I know people are angry they aren't getting 100% of my time and attention any more, but I just can't keep this up." A workshop participant shared how they had tried, unsuccessfully, to shift the amount of time they spent in community organizations, "People kept asking me to do things, attend events even after I said no. They kept wearing me down and, eventually, I gave in." Pressure to participate may get us in the room more, but how is the quality of our activism diminished when we continually push ourselves to show up, even when we are ever so close to passion fatigue and burnout?

Self-sabotage

"Caring for myself is not self-indulgence, it is self-preservation, and that is an act of political warfare."

~ Audre Lorde

My hope is this powerful quote from Audre Lorde has brought you needed reassurance and support when you have questioned if you were being selfish and self-centered for taking some time for rest and renewal. It is critical that we center self-care in our lives so we have the necessary energy, clarity, and patience to be effective change agents. As one of my clients said as they reflected on the direct connection between self-care and activism, "I understand self-care as cultivating compassion for myself and others. When I am more centered, I respond with far greater passion, compassion, and effectiveness. I am a far better change agent. Self-care is essential for effective social change work."

My fear is that too many change agents and activists, including myself, only give lip service to self-care as we continue to push ourselves and over-do in our own lives. We often may encourage and support others to focus on themselves so they can stay energized and passionate in their activism and change work, but how often do we follow our own advice?

There are so many ways we sabotage our own health and self-care, most are rooted in our thoughts. Can you relate to ever thinking these fears: If I stop for even a short time, I will lose momentum; I'm letting others down; I'll disappoint my friends and colleagues; People will get angry with me; I'll be colluding; I'm letting down the cause. If I don't do it, who will? What will people think of me?

One workshop participant's comments illustrate how guilt and shame can be debilitating, powerful drivers for over-working, "I drive myself to over-do. I think I always have to be productive. I always have to be working. I feel guilty if I just sit and do nothing for an hour or two. Even if I am watching TV, I feel

I have to be scrolling through Facebook and repost social justice news and articles."

Even if we know we need more healthy ways to replenish ourselves, sometimes we don't. As one client said, "The resistance and backlash come from me. I just have so little time or energy that I can't even imagine doing anything that is taking care of myself like eating better, working out, or socializing with friends. I just want to sleep for days and binge a season of 'Law & Order'."

The pressures to over-work and put ourselves last are so intense. It is easy to just keep doing what we have been doing and hope we don't burn out before the next planned break in our schedule. If you are like me, I need to be constantly aware of the costs to others and to myself if I don't take good care of myself. I need a deeply compelling reason to make and maintain more healthy choices in my life or I will easily slide back into old, familiar patterns of over-doing, sacrificing myself in the process.

Costs of NOT Centering Self-Care in Our Lives

Passion fatigue

"Working hard for something we don't care about is called stress. Working hard for something we love is called passion."

~ Unknown Author

Many of us experience increasing stress as we work on projects and attend meetings about topics in which we have minimal investment. At the same time, we keep pushing our limits to create greater equity and inclusion in our organizations and in society while also juggling so many other, often competing, demands. Unfortunately, at some point, many of us cross a seemingly invisible line into the burnout zone and find ourselves caring less and less for what we used to feel such deep, unrelenting passion.

Can you relate to ever feeling more apathetic? Have you ever stopped caring as much and started to just go through the motions in social change work? Where many of us used to feel such passion and commitment, we now just feel debilitating stress from all the hard work of creating change.

I know this place of passion fatigue and believe many activists and change agents experience this loss of enthusiasm and commitment to the cause. As one workshop participant said, "I feel far less energy, passion, and joy in the work. Without these, it feels like a chore." Another said, "I'm not giving my best any more, or even something close to it. I just can't get up the energy. All I see is another time-sucking opportunity."

Another cost of passion fatigue is we find ourselves questioning our usefulness more often. As one participant noted in a workshop, "I want to make such an impact in my life, but at this point, I'm not sure I make much of a difference even when I do show up."

Passion fatigue and all the stress and pressure of social change work not only impact us as individuals, but also undermine team effectiveness. So many groups experience increasingly unproductive tension and conflict as members express greater frustration and criticism about others in the group and its leaders. These dysfunctional group dynamics often result in stagnation and ineffectiveness. The increasing sense of pessimism, hopelessness, and despair from a lack of progress and success can severely impact retention of both group members and leaders.

As a result of passion fatigue, we begin to pull back. One client noted, "I began to skip task force meetings and other committee work to avoid hearing more about how bad things are or possibly getting assigned another task to complete." Without an intentional intervention and a chance for meaningful dialogue about self-care and activism, people will stop out and even drop out. Over time, many change efforts suffer as leaders and members dwindle away, and, possibly never come back.

How many initiatives in your organization and local community have failed because of the loss of membership? As more people slow down or drop out, many groups no longer have enough people with the necessary stamina, bandwidth, and competencies to truly shift oppressive organizations and societal structures. They no longer have enough people committed to staying in it for the long haul. Without sustainable change efforts, unless we can continue to attract, nurture, develop, and retain the next wave, the next generations of passionate change agents, then the cycles of oppression continue to win and no real, sustainable movement ever occurs.

Can you relate to feeling so guilty for not showing up as fully as before, yet hoping you can convince yourself it doesn't matter? If you are like many change agents I know, you beat yourself up for stopping out and continue to feel overwhelmed and exhausted by all that needs to change.

"The trouble is that once you see it, you can't unsee it.
And once you've seen it, keeping quiet, saying nothing,

becomes as political an act as speaking out. There is no innocence. Either way, you are accountable."

~ Arundhati Roy

Impact at work

When we are experiencing high stress and early burnout, our productivity suffers. The quality of our work diminishes as we make more careless mistakes, produce sloppier work, and waste time having to redo and revise projects and reports. We may find we under-perform as we cut more corners and do only as much as we think is required to stay under our supervisor's radar. We might start to delegate key responsibilities that we really should be doing ourselves. While this may initially feel like a stretch opportunity for direct reports, they may soon come to resent our leadership and feel over-burdened as they do our work for us.

When deeply stressed, we often react unproductively in difficult situations and damage working relationships. Our triggered reactions can often alienate others and take precious time and energy to rebuild trust and effective working relationships, if we ever can. One client shared a particularly powerful example:

"I was losing sleep, attached to my devices, and pushing myself so hard I didn't make any quality time for important relationships in my life or the things that bring me joy and rejuvenation. Things came to a head when the people I supervised shared how they were feeling unheard, not supported, and devalued in their roles on the team. This finally got my attention. It was hard and humbling to realize the negative impact of my lack of self- care and well-being on people I valued and cared about."

As another client noted, "I get overly focused on transactions and products, and forget how critical dialogue, engagement, and process are in the change work." While we may be able to repair the negative damage to working relationships, sometimes we can't. One participant talked about their triggered impact on one of their direct reports:

"I was so stressed out from trying to lead my team through some significant organizational change. I was so distracted and consumed by my dramas that when a staff member tried to share with me about some significant life challenges she was facing, I came across as far more uncaring and impersonal than I ever want to be. As a result, she is far less trusting of me and we haven't been able to rebuild a good working relationship yet."

Another related negative impact is we model burned out leadership for employees. As a result, they may feel the need to take on more than is reasonably possible and over-stretch themselves. They may put in more face-time out of fear they will be reprimanded and thought to be poor performers if they don't match the frenetic level of activity of their supervisors and leaders.

High stress, high producing environments create other unproductive results such as employee negativity and low morale. As one workshop participant described, "When I am more centered, I can rise above the toxic workplace dynamics that often occur. I can stay on course. When I am more stressed and my attitude is off, I find myself stooping to the toxic levels of others, helping to escalate the negative dynamics by perpetuating the unproductive gossip and negativity." It is common for employees to lose their patience, empathy, and compassion when they are burning out. As one client remarked, "I don't listen well and become much more direct and blunt with others. I also have a far lower threshold for special cases or individual needs and become easily frustrated with them. People easily notice my lack of compassion and empathy."

Some recent workshop participants talked about routinely feeling defeated, deflated, and unmotivated in stressful, toxic work environments, "I lose creativity, innovative ideas. I am much more judgmental and negative and only see the problems and challenges. And my energy is contagious. I watch others lose their spark and motivation like I am an anchor pulling everyone down with me." In a related comment, another participant in the session described how they could become more insistent, self-righteous, and arrogant when they were highly stressed: "I keep pushing my own ideas over and over, becoming the difficult situation others have to navigate."

While some, like me, may get more arrogant when we push ourselves, others may at times begin to doubt themselves and lose confidence in their abilities. As a few clients have noted, they began to question if they should not only quit their job, but also leave their field. They wondered if they should find something far less stressful and demanding, not only because of the impact of stress in their lives, but also because they questioned if they really had the competence and capacity to do the work.

Burnout and passion fatigue can impact our career development. One client wondered:

"I just have a feeling, I can't prove it, but I have a sense that my boss didn't recommend me for a very visible task force because of how I have been reacting lately. I missed a chance to be on a committee with several top leaders which would have really helped them know what I do and my breadth of capacity. But I think my supervisor has been put off by my recent irritability and melt downs. He recommended someone who always seems positive, though isn't a critical thinker, in my opinion."

Another client shared a similar impact on their career, "I miss opportunities to be of greater service, to learn new skills and approaches. If I'm too stressed out, I might miss opportunities to advance my career." A related consequence can have far-reaching impact on our change work. A number of people I have worked with described the pressure from management to cut back on their social justice work. One client told me, "When I burn out, my supervisor attributes it to my social justice activities and gets more critical of the ways I work to create greater inclusion in the organization. Lately, she has pressured me to cut back."

Physical and mental health

One of the most common costs of burnout and passion fatigue is our personal health. As one client noted, "I just feel so fatigued, so tired all the time. I'm so exhausted that I don't have time to reflect, re-center, dream, or think about new ideas or plans." One way many people seem to compensate for this level of fatigue is to over-use caffeine and sugar in order to feel they have more energy or drink alcohol and use other drugs to relax and de-stress after a long day. Add to these dynamics the common pattern of eating on the run in this grab-and-go culture and many people find their poor eating habits deplete their energy. After a sugary, high carb and high fat meal, many feel more tired and depleted, run down and lethargic. Some may experience other consequences like this training participant who noted, "I stress eat and then gain weight, and then beat myself up for being heavy."

Burnout, stress, and these common lifestyle choices deplete our immune systems. Many people report getting sick right at the end of a major push, such as the end of a semester, a big project, or a major activist campaign. In the beginning of our careers, many seem able to usually get enough rest over a long weekend or during winter or spring break to bounce back and continue their pace and intensity of work. Over time, my guess is more and more people are like me. I started to get sick more often and had trouble getting over a cold or flu in a few days. It would linger while I started back to work, only to come down with another virus or bacterial infection. We think we are saving time by not stopping to take better care of ourselves, when in reality we lose so much momentum, productivity, and quality of work by being out sick or working at half-speed for a week or two until we get better.

One workshop participant talked about the impact of stress on their health, "I have chronic fatigue and these symptoms become exaggerated as I approach my wall. As I have become more aware of the subtle physical, mental, spiritual, and emotional changes or signals that preceded major warning signs, I have been able to intervene more quickly to shift my life before I go over the edge."

While some may disagree, I believe that neglecting my self-care and health in the moment will contribute to my experiencing serious illness in the future. When I share this in a session, someone inevitably talks about their 95-year old aunt who lived a full life drinking bourbon, smoking, and eating sugar and red meat until the day she dropped dead. That may be true for some people. I just know I am not one of them. I have too many stories of getting sick from over-working or eating sugar and wheat. I'd much rather be intentional now than sorry later.

Living a more balanced, healthy lifestyle now may be even more critical for the increasing numbers of people I meet who have a family history of heart conditions, asthma, diabetes, cancer, and other conditions which suggest they may be more susceptible to these diseases. As you know, research consistently points to the significant increases in these diseases and others in groups which experience marginalization in the U.S.

I am grateful for the public dialogue about issues of mental health, even though I still see and hear so many oppressive comments and organizational structures that negatively impact those with some type of mental illness. Numerous participants in my workshops talk about how they live with anxiety, depression, or some other mental health issue. They were clear that if they hadn't heeded the early warning signs of burnout and started to take better care of themselves immediately, they could have experienced very serious, debilitating consequences in their lives.

Relationships

Our relationships at work, home, and in our communities suffer when we are experiencing burnout and passion fatigue. One parent's comment summarized many that I've heard in sessions:

"When I do not take care of myself, I can't show up for the important relationships in my life. I put my kids and partner's needs on the back burner while I address work issues. When I get home, my youngest child asks, "Do you have homework or work to do tonight?" It breaks my heart. I fear they will look back on these years and resent that I wasn't around more, engaged more."

When we are increasingly busy at work and in community organizations, our intimate relationships suffer as well. As a client mentioned, "When I am stressed about how much there is to do, I tend to stay longer at work which causes problems between me and my partner." We lose some of the sense of connectedness and harmony in our relationships and often experience more conflict and tension as we get out of sync with each other. Too often, we try to handle it all by ourselves and we keep going until we collapse and crash. At that point, we are of little use to anyone, even ourselves.

Benefits of Self-Care

I am at my best as a change agent when I am rested, centered, and grounded enough to think clearly. The enormous costs of ignoring our self-care may be enough for some people to find compelling reasons to change their lives. It might also be useful to identify the significant benefits of focusing on our health and self-care as social justice change agents.

I was mesmerized by a Facebook post of someone who appeared to be a 5-year old girl in utter joy and delight as she played in a sprinkler on a hot day. The caption read, "Remember her? She is still there…inside you, waiting…let's go get her." Like me, do you have faint memories of feeling free and spontaneously playful? Of being a young child without all the shoulds, rules, and demands of the socialization we experience as adults? I yearn to uncover and reveal this spirited being.

Self-care is awakening to the numbing and soul-destroying impact of societal messaging so we can reclaim our true, life-filled, love-filled selves. We need to defy the judgments, put-downs, and recriminations of others and stay true to our inner vision of who we want to be, who we really are. It may take time to find this part of ourselves again, but it is definitely still there.

We need to learn how to be free of that chorus of negative messages in our minds: "Work till you drop; Your work proves how worthwhile you are; Nobody can do it as good as you; and, Exhaustion is a sign you are doing good work."

Contrary to all these oppressive messages, change teams and community groups are far more effective and productive when members have the vitality and creativity to imagine new, innovative solutions and can engage in productive dialogue and disagreement without debilitating triggers and difficult situations draining the life force of the group. Effective change work requires a depth of patience and clear thinking that I only have when I am more grounded and peaceful in my heart.

In one of the first research studies to explore the impact of mindfulness self-care practices on activist burnout, Paul Gorski found that self-care not only helped change agents mitigate their burnout symptoms, but also helped them sustain their activism and show up as more effective activists as they engaged the work with greater clarity, thoughtfulness, patience, and compassion (Gorski, 2015).

I feel greater hope when I hear clients describe the benefits of focusing on their self-care:

"As I started to take better care of myself, I had more energy and passion to make changes in our organization. I got involved in a sexuality and gender allies initiative that was not only helpful to the organization but has become a source of rejuvenation, support, and hope for myself as well."

One workshop participant shared how self-care helped them in their change work as a member of multiple privileged groups:

"I am much more present and thoughtful as I choose how to engage and respond, so I react less in ways that cause harm or leave people triggered by my actions. When I am centered, I am able to better anticipate needs of others, especially those in marginalized identities, as we explore how decisions could negatively impact people across various marginalized groups."

Another participant recognized a direct correlation between self-care and their effectiveness in a very difficult situation:

"The president, in response to students pushing back about lack of faculty of color on campus, defended his actions saying he was trying to change this. If I had been exhausted in that moment, I would have felt deeply triggered and would have disregarded him as another clueless white leader. Instead, I was able to acknowledge his intent and some of the productive actions to date and ask the students different questions, which helped the president come up with more useful responses. We were able to build more understanding and connectedness in that open forum as we explored specific ideas for change as a community. My inner balance helped me stay engaged instead of reacting out of my trauma and triggers."

I wish I had people in my life like the previous change agent who could have modelled how to be a powerful, passionate change agent without burning out. I could have used their advice and coaching as they shared ways to create a more balanced life that helped them sustain their effectiveness as a change agent over the long haul. I can't go back and get what I needed in the past, but I can be far more focused and intentional today to develop the tools, willingness, and capacity to infuse self-care practices into my daily life. My challenge was I didn't know how to change my life. In the next two chapters, I explore a wide variety of helpful techniques and tools to help you lead a more stress-free, productive life as an effective social justice change agent.

CHAPTER 5

Tips and Tools to Add More Self-Care to Your Life

Progress, not perfection

L et me just say, there is nothing like writing a book on self-care to get you to look closely at your own life, past and present! I recently came home from an amazing experience at the White Privilege Conference. I was pumped and excited by the conversations and insights I was gifted with throughout the three days I was presenting and participating in sessions. The morning after I returned from the conference, I woke up in a pretty good mood and went into my office to reply to some emails and pay some bills. I noticed a couple irregularities in the credit card bill and easily took care of the issue as I talked with a representative. As I moved on to follow-up with the cable company, I soon realized I was not in a good place to be putting myself in the path of potential conflict. After hitting several obstacles and asking to speak with a supervisor three times in hopes they could help resolve the issue, and then being told no each time, I was so frustrated and knew I needed to end the call still live up to my core value of "do no harm."

As I hung up, I realized I had created this whole stressful dynamic by launching back into running my business without taking enough of a break to rest and refuel from the conference. Even though it had been a fabulous experience, I expended far more energy and reserves than I had realized. I should have blocked off that Sunday for rest, re-connecting with my wife, and refueling with a nap and a long walk in nature. In this chapter, I highlight a wide range of tools and strategies to add more self-care in our lives. These tips have helped me organize and navigate the world around me as I make better choices to center my own well-being.

> *"Everything that is happening at this moment is a result of the choices you've made in the past."*
>
> ~ Deepak Chopra

While some may not agree with this quote as it applies to life tragedies, when it comes to our general level of self-care, burnout, and exhaustion, I do believe the level of fatigue and depletion I felt as I talked with the cable company was directly related to the choices I had made. Each individual decision to attend a conference or schedule another training trip or agree to make another speech seemed reasonable and doable in the moment I made each commitment. What I realize now is that I hadn't taken a step back and looked at the full picture of my life as I made each individual choice. In a period of about eight weeks, I had planned to attend four conferences, had booked numerous training sessions, and had agreed to develop and give a new keynote address. All the while knowing that we had to pack up and move our entire lives across the country, all with a broken wrist!

The good news is I didn't berate and judge myself when I realized how exhausted I had become and how I had created this situation for myself, again. I viewed that triggering moment with the cable service provider as a gentle wake-up call to pay much more attention to my seemingly discreet, independent choices as I make decisions about how I use my time and life energy. I was reminded, again, of the critical need to take an eagle's view of my life as I make each decision. They are not individual choices, but part of an inter-connected web of my life. Remembering to schedule in self-care and downtime on my calendar as easily as I book a training or coaching session helps me create and live the life I envision.

> *"Make a difference about something other than yourselves."*
>
> ~ Toni Morrison

Like so many activists and change agents, I have had a fire in my belly since a young age, a drive to make a difference in the world. But over time, I began to question if I could really make any significant difference in the world and not be exhausted all the time. I wondered how I would be able to help others, if I could barely manage my own life. In order to sustain our capacity and passion to create meaningful change, I believe we all need more than the original 3 R's in our lives. We need these R's: Rest, Refill, Reflect, Reprioritize, Rejuvenate, and Revolutionize.

Rest

*"You have permission to rest. You are not
responsible for fixing everything that is broken. You
do not have to try and make everyone happy. For
now, take time for you. It's time to replenish."*

~ Unknown Author

I was facilitating a training session and heard some say they needed "deep rest". Only later did I realize they had said they were "depressed". When I am exhausted, feeling hopeless, and questioning the value of my activism, it is a clear sign I need deep rest, though I am usually resistant to taking a break. When our reserves are empty and we are dragging ourselves out of bed to take on another day, we deeply need to reorder our lives and take time for rest.

*"Each person deserves a day away in which no
problems are confronted, no solutions searched for.
Each of us needs to withdraw from the cares which
will not withdraw from us."*

~ Maya Angelou

Some people unplug from social media and take a few days to sleep and connect with family and friends. Others tune out the news and commit to not checking their emails or doing any computer work for the weekend. Some take a long weekend or vacation or even a staycation, and set their intention to take a complete break from everything that is draining in their lives.

For me, it is important that I not simply substitute endless fun activities into my day or I will feel as exhausted as before, just with a lot of lovely memories. Taking long, uninterrupted naps is such a joyful way for me to rest. Just as a field needs times of fallow to re-nourish so plants will flourish in the new season so, too, we need fallow, down times.

"Life is all about balance. You don't always need to get stuff done. Sometimes it's perfectly ok, and absolutely necessary, to shut down, kick back and do nothing."

~ Lori Deschene

I still resist this message to kick back and do nothing for a while. My fear is that I won't start back up again. I have memories of stopping out for periods of time and how difficult it was for me to get refocused and re-energized again. On reflection, I realize those times in my life occurred when I was in deep burnout and passion fatigue, such as after I completed my doctorate or at the end of a very challenging semester in a toxic work environment. I never really learned how to rest and take regular short breaks. If I had, I might have prevented all those times I unconsciously slid into burnout. The key may be to learn to stop to rest and then get back in the game. Though, there may be times we need a far longer rest, possibly a period of hibernation.

"Although for most of my teaching career the university classroom has been an exhilarating place, in recent years I have begun to feel a need for significant time away from my job. I was burning out. Entering the classroom at the big city university where I taught,

*I began to feel as though I was entering a prison,
a closed-down space where, no matter how hard I
tried, it was difficult to create a positive context for
learning...In actuality, these obstacles had always been
a part of my teaching experience. My capacity to cope
with them in a constructive way was diminishing. I
needed time away from teaching."*

~ bell hooks

I wish we all had access to a sabbatical program similar to ones available to many tenured-track faculty at most colleges and universities. Every seven or so years, they have the opportunity to take a 6-12 month break from teaching to focus on their passion. Many may use this time to travel, do some research, complete some writing projects, or revise their course syllabi. Can you imagine if all organizational structures were changed to support people taking an intentional break to rest and recreate themselves? As bell hooks so powerfully shared, there are times we need and deserve a more intensive rest and break from our life's work so we come back with greater clarity of purpose and renewed energy to be of service. Usually, this requires time to replenish ourselves, our reserves.

Refill

As I was coming out in my early 20's, I immersed myself in the music of Cris Williamson. Her songs and lyrics sustained me through some incredibly difficult times in my life. In a part of the chorus from her song, *Waterfall*, she talked about the need to keep filling up and spilling over like a waterfall. Rest is critical for our self-care, and so is the time to refill our stores of energy and passion so we have the resources to more consistently fuel our change work over time.

What do you do to replenish and restore yourself to be of greater service? Some people might put on their favorite music as they get their hands in the earth and garden. Others may hike in the mountains or dance around the kitchen as they lovingly prepare a sumptuous meal for family and friends. I started playing the guitar again and I feel more renewed after I sing along with my old friends James Taylor, John Denver, and Carole King.

Many find a regular yoga or meditation practice helps them to refill their empty buckets. Morning journaling after reflecting on inspirational readings can replenish our souls as we prepare to go to work. When I have a consistent work out each day, I find I have so much more energy to invest in my social change work.

The tricky part is some activities may look and feel like they are refilling us, when they are just coping techniques or may actually be draining us as well. Binging on a few movies or a season of *House of Cards* may feel restful, but may not be refilling. Often after I zone out on certain types of shows or videos, I realize I don't feel as replenished as I had hoped or needed. Choosing to check out for a while or distract ourselves from stressors in our lives can give us a break, but most likely won't refill us. Coping can be useful, but we may find we are more grounded and have greater clarity if we intentionally choose activities that emotionally fill us up as well. I am in a far different mood and energy space if I watch an uplifting movie as compared to a few TV dramas filled with violence and death. They may be an enjoyable distraction, but usually not restorative.

"I'm used to people saying to me, 'Wow, your self-care is so good!' I always look at them blankly. I never think of what I do—cooking good food for myself on my budget that supports my body and my chronic illness, going to working-class acupuncture twice a month, stretching, drinking a lot of herbs, making sure I get sleep—as 'self-care'. I think of it as the stuff I do to love myself in a fucked-up world, that helps me have more days with less pain, and helps me give my body love when I'm having days with a lot of pain and fatigue."

~ Leah Lakshmi Piepzna-Samarasinha

It is critical that we each take an honest assessment of our needs and plan regular times to take care of ourselves and restore our health and energy levels so we have the capacity to continue to show up in service as change agents.

Reflect

"Quit saying you don't have time. You have time for what you make time for in life."

~ Bryant McGill

Activity: How I currently spend my time and energy

I still bristle when I read this quote. My life can feel so out of control at times. Yet, I do believe that we have time for things when we make the time. I remember having an unexpected insight as I tried out an activity I'd designed for a self-care workshop. I encourage you to take a moment and complete this activity as I share my experience. I developed a worksheet to help people get a more accurate account of how they spend their time. You can download it from my website, www.drkathyobear.com/selfcare On the left-hand side of the worksheet I invite people to list all of their common activities for both a typical work day and a day-off, including meetings, phone calls, project development, transportation, shopping, cleaning, preparing and eating food, exercise, time with family and their intimate partner, socializing with friends, watching TV, social media, parenting, sleeping, religious/spiritual practices, etc. I then ask them to assign how much time they generally would spend on each activity in a typical day, knowing every day is somewhat unique.

Having to quantify and account for our time can be a powerful awareness tool. The next step can help us get even greater clarity. I then ask people to create a visual image of their use of time by drawing in their activities on two rulers: One for a workday and one for a day off. Each ruler is divided into 24 "inches" with each inch representing an hour of time. For instance, I usually sleep eight hours a night, so I would color in 8 inches and write "sleep" next to that section. Most workdays, I am at my desk developing resources or on coaching calls for another eight hours each day, so I would fill that in. I got new insight as I colored in the rest of what I typically do and realized I still had a couple hours left over that I wasn't clear how I used. I know I definitely filled up each day, but I realized I wasn't always intentional or aware of how I spent my time.

Take a moment and complete this activity www.drkathyobear. com/selfcare. Then reflect on your rulers and notice how you currently spend your time. Where do you invest your energy? In working, your physical health and fitness, healthy eating, nurturing relationships? Where are you "losing time" to stressing out, unproductive conversations and activities, doing low priority tasks in high thinking times, or doing high priority tasks in low energy times? What activities bring you energy? Which deplete you? How does everything you do contribute to your life goals? Or not? It may be useful to spend the next week taking notes every 30-60 minutes of how you are using your time on workdays and days off. This more accurate accounting may bring you even more insights.

A key step to greater self-care is deepening your awareness and attention of how you are currently living your life by noticing the choices you make and how you invest your time and energy. If you are like me, this helped me get a clearer picture of the impact of my life choices on others and myself. Our current reality is the inevitable result of a multitude of choices we made, some consciously and others on automatic pilot. Some willingly and, possibly, many with resentment or feelings of obligation. Once we increase our awareness, we can make different choices that might better help us rest and refill. The next step is to assess how satisfied we are with each aspect of our lives.

Activity: How satisfied are you with different aspects of your life?

It takes courage to be willing to look honestly at your life and recognize what is working and what is not, to identify the dysfunctional ways we choose to live that undermine our capacity to create long-term sustainable change in the world. Most of the time, I believe we don't want to know, so we don't take the time to reflect and examine our lives. With wishful thinking, we keep pushing ourselves past what is reasonable, hoping that maybe this time we won't crash and burn.

Take a pause from reading to complete the worksheet, *How Satisfied Are You?* on my website www.drkathyobear.com/selfcare. Use a scale from 0-10, not at all to completely, to rate each of the eighteen areas, including work life, career, physical health, life dreams, fitness, emotional and mental health, eating and sleeping patterns, time with family and friends, your intimate relationship, time for rest and play, spiritual practices, financial health, and ways you are of service. While this may feel like an extensive list, feel free to add more areas of your life to explore. Reflect back on your ratings and note where you feel the most satisfied in your life and which areas may need more of your time and attention.

Activity: Envision the life you want

"The first step to getting somewhere is to decide you are not going to stay where you are."

~ J.P. Morgan

Increasing our awareness is a critical step. We then need to decide how we want to live differently. A good place to start is to imagine more about the life we want to lead. When I was training to be a Life Coach with Dr. Martha Beck, I learned several tools that my clients find very useful to get more clarity about the future they want to create. The tool *Ideal Day* is a great way to get in touch with your deeper yearnings and visions for a more balanced life. After getting clients more grounded and meditative, I ask them to envision waking up in the morning on their ideal day. As I take notes, they talk me through the specific details of where they are, who they are with, how they are feeling, and the various things they do as they are waking up and getting ready for the day. As we move through the rest of the day, some are surprised that they live in a different location or have a different job or have new and different people in their lives. Most find they are less busy and frenetic and take more time to enjoy their lives and the people around them. After the meditation is complete, they reflect on their visualization and identify aspects of their ideal day they want to bring more into their current life.

With some clients, I use a variation of the *Ideal Day* meditation, to help them visualize their *Ideal Job*. I invite them to imagine their lives in 3-5 years as they are getting ready and then starting to work. I invite them to notice where they are, what they are doing, and with whom they are interacting. People often get new insights into how they want to live and work differently.

Another tool I learned in the Life Coaching Program with Martha Beck is the *Vision Board*. I like this technique because it gives me a tangible set of images I can post on my wall and revisit regularly. To get ready, gather a bunch of magazines and get into a quiet, meditative space. Take multiple long, deep breaths as you focus on a key question in your life, like: How do I want to live my life? What are the aspects of my best life? or How can I be of greatest service? Then, start to flip through the magazines and notice what pictures, graphics, words, and phrases jump out at you. Tear these out and make a pile for later. Don't worry if you're not always sure what they mean in the moment. Insights will appear for you at the right time. You may want to stay open to messages that come to you even after you finish looking through the magazines.

I often get insights for my vision boards from billboards or someone wearing a t-shirt and even from TV commercials. Once you feel you have a full set of materials, you can begin to create your vision board using tape or glue and a piece of poster board. Many find it useful to talk through their vision board with someone in their life while others choose to keep their board a private affair. It may be useful to journal after you complete your board to collect up your thoughts and feelings as well as take time to sit with your vision board every week to see what new insights you gather and how you can shift your current life activities to better align with your vision of your future.

> *"If you don't know where you are going, any road will get you there."*
>
> ~ Lewis Carroll

In order to lead a more balanced life, we must first reflect as we develop a clear image and vision of what we want. Then, we need to make a commitment to live differently as we create what we envision and manifest our future, today. To do this, we have to learn how to reprioritize.

Reprioritize

> *"If you don't have time for what matters, stop doing things that don't."*
>
> ~ Courtney Carver

This is where I often get stuck. I just want to be able to do more of what I want to do while I also keep doing everything else in my life. I balk at saying no or letting go of things that no longer serve me as much as they used to. I may feel obligated or I really enjoy doing something, but find it increasingly exhausting especially when it doesn't add much value to my life goals. These are hard choices for me and my guess is they are for you as well.

Assess activities against your life goals

As I get more clarity about the vision of my ideal life, my passions, and my calling, I can then use these as benchmarks against which I measure each and every choice I make about how I use my time. I can ask myself: "Is this bringing me closer to my goals?" "Will this help me be of greater service in ways that do not severely deplete me?" "Do I feel joy and in the flow when I do this?" "Will this help me learn how to create more effective change in the world?" "Will this help me rest, refill, and refuel in ways that are healthy and sustaining?"

I enjoy doing many different things, but I realized that sometimes I was investing more of myself in areas that were not aligned with my higher goals. And more importantly, I was outside of my zone of genius, my super powers. I love these terms that are being discussed in the mainstream these days. I used to think I had to take every job offer and work with whomever wanted to hire me. Today, I realize I am far more effective when I work within what I do well, my zone of genius, the place where I feel energized and in the flow. There are so many others who can work with organizations that are in stages of development that are now outside of where I believe I can make the most impact. I used to feel guilty for saying no and turning down work. Now, I believe the people I recommend or the consultants they find on their own may be far better positioned to be useful for that organization.

I can't help or save everyone and believing that I could or even that I should was actually a major part of the problem. I spent years over-helping and over-pleasing in hopes that people would like me, would be my friend. And, I got a false ego-hit every time I felt I helped or fixed or saved someone. These moments gave my life an artificial sense of purpose. I was building my sense of self on shifting sands, or more accurately, quicksand. I gave myself away and lost more of myself every time I participated in these unhealthy dynamics. Eventually, I felt so miserable and spiritually bankrupt that I felt deep resentment and rage toward everyone I had "helped". I blamed them for sucking the life out of me. In all of these situations, I got to believe I was the blameless martyr who selfishly gave to others who never appreciated me.

Today, I have greater self-care when I first check-in with my body and spirit to see how or if I am available to be useful and then offer what I do out of love and care, without any strings or expectations attached. I do it for me, not for others. And sometimes, the most loving thing I can do is to choose acceptance and detachment - of where they are, of their life choices, and send them love and light as I move along on my journey.

What are your super powers? What are your strengths? What do you enjoy doing and find soul-filling that contributes to sustainable social change in organizations and society? I believe we each are on this earth this time with special talents and gifts to share. We are here to learn and to make a difference in the world. What is your gift to the world? When I stay in my zone of genius, I am in the flow. I feel more alive, time passes without my noticing, and I am of far greater service to others than when I am doing things that are not my super powers. In fact, when

I am out of my zone, I am often more tired, irritable, and easily triggered and so my reactions can undermine what I am intending to create. Identify your zone of genius and plan how to spend more time there. This may require letting go of many things that you once valued.

Accept you are not as young as you once were

In order to reprioritize, I had to be willing to recognize and admit I had limits and that I can no longer try to do everything I want to do at full speed. I'm not as young and energetic as I used to be. This is not an easy realization to accept. I want to believe that I can still do it all, yet I have countless evidence that my body and energy stores have shifted with age.

The good news is I am discovering innovative ways to streamline and focus my efforts so that I am actually making a far greater difference in the world than before, just differently than I used to. Accepting my new reality and letting go of past expectations have both been critical steps in this renewal process. I feel re-energized as I refocus on how I can be of greatest service in my current life situation. I believe I can sustain my passion and impact over the years as I continue to reassess and re-prioritize my goals and strategies given my shifting levels of energy and physical capacity.

Get clear on your priorities

As I prepare to start work each day, I look at my to-do list and decide what is my priority for the day, or even for the morning. I get clear on what rises to the top for me in that moment and know that not everything is urgent or critical, just because someone else thinks it is. I need to listen to my inner self and block out all the noise and demands from others. I keep my eyes on my goals and assess how each potential task will help me serve others and create greater inclusion and social justice. This frame gives me permission to make choices, say no, and not feel guilty. As one workshop participant noted, we need to reprioritize:

"When everything is a priority, nothing is. Some things are nice to have, but not essential or central to my work. By choosing where to put my focus, I have more pride in my work because I have better results from investing quality attention and time. This fuels me to keep going."

The Body Compass

Reprioritizing often requires that we start saying "no" more often. I used to and can still feel very guilty when I say no or turn down a request. I feel selfish and self-centered. Yet, if I say yes to everything, I rarely am very useful for very long. Studying with Martha Beck, I learned a few more techniques that help me decide where to put my energy, when to say yes, and when to say no. *The Body Compass* is an amazing tool to help me access information as I make decisions. Clients find this a powerful way to quiet their minds and let their bodies give them insights.

To use the body compass to decide how to live in greater balance, first get into a quiet, relaxed state and close your eyes. Then imagine a very stressful situation and replay it over in your mind's eye a few times. Remember who was there, what was said, and who did what. When you feel you are fully back in that moment, scan your body and notice every sensation and emotion you are experiencing. Then assign a rating to this physical and emotional state using a scale from -10 (I never want to experience this again) to +10 (bring me more of this!). If you are like most people who rate a very stressful situation, you may find these body sensations and emotions feel around a -4 to -10.

In coaching sessions, I then ask clients to literally stand up and shake off this memory and these body sensations. I often will do a happy dance along with them as they release these emotions. After a few deep, cleansing breaths, I have the client remember a situation where they felt deep joy and happiness at work or in the rest of their life. I have them mentally replay that event several times. When they are ready, I ask them to scan their bodies and describe their sensations. Instead of tension, aches, and tightness which people often experience in the first memory, most feel much lighter, pain-free, and able to breathe deeply. When I ask them to assign a rating to these body sensations and emotions, they often choose between a +5 to +10.

At this point, they are now able to use their bodies to assess how stressful or joyful various situations are and could be. It can be as simple as imagining completing a task or going to an event and rating the body sensations, thoughts, and emotions that arise. I find that when I feel joy and excitement as I'm exploring the possibility of taking on a particular training or coaching opportunity, I am more likely to do a better job and feel I am being of service. However, when I agree to do something even if I had warning signals when I considered doing the task, signs like low energy or a tight chest or slight irritation, then I more often do not enjoy the work and, as a result, might not be as effective as I had hoped. When I fill my life with activities and experiences that I imagine to be on the positive end of the body compass scale, I feel far less depleted and exhausted over time.

"What I really have to prioritize is self-care, something as basic as getting sleep. I've had to say no to a lot of things. There's a cost for me emotionally when I speak up about things. I'm always a target because I'm a public figure, and I'm not doing activism in obscurity. I have to get myself ready for the bullets."

~ Laverne Cox

I dearly appreciate these insights from Laverne Cox. My guess is most of us are unaware of the draining costs of our activism and social change work as we put ourselves on the line, in the line of fire. While possibly not to the extent she experiences, we all may face situations that seriously deplete us. Without an intentional plan for self-care and renewal, without carefully choosing where and how to invest ourselves in this work, we may end up burning out over and over, without making much of a positive difference along the way.

Setting boundaries

A client once talked about the connection between self-care and success, "I have cut back, said 'no' more, and now have more energy and capacity to focus on the elements of my work that drive student success." While it may feel hard to do, saying no and reprioritizing can give us more capacity to do far more meaningful work in sustainable ways. As Brené Brown reminds us:

"Compassionate people ask for what they need. They say no when they need to, and when they say

yes, they mean it. They're compassionate because
their boundaries keep them out of resentment."

~ Brené Brown

I used to get so angry and upset when people violated my boundaries. Can you hear the victim language in my thought? I had loose boundaries and then blamed others when I felt their behavior crossed a line. I made up very unproductive stories like, "They took advantage of my generosity," "She betrayed my trust," and "He doesn't appreciate me or value all that I do!" I love this quote from Sonya Parker:

"People know who they can walk over and who they
can't. If someone is walking all over you it's because
they know you'll put up with it."

~ Sonya Parker

In the past, people walked all over me because I let them. To change my behavior, I had to first realize why I created such loose boundaries and learn to value myself as much as I valued others. I needed to believe I deserved to take care of myself and not have people cross my boundaries. Next, I needed to develop the courage and the skills to speak up, to speak my truth to power. I find this a spiral path of growth for me. I do better some days, in some areas, and then fall short at other times. As long as I stay committed to the process, I am strengthening my capacity and building new habits of self-care, one day at a time. And in the process, I hope I am beginning to model, as so many have before, another way of creating change in the world.

Activity: Create a Depletion Map

"People inspire you or they drain you. Pick them wisely."

~ Hans F. Hansen

If I use the body compass after every activity and interaction with someone, I begin to notice a pattern of times I feel filled and times I feel more depleted. It may be useful for you to make a Depletion Map and sketch out people and events that are typically draining as well as those that are refilling for you. I have only so much emotional, physical, and spiritual energy to expend each day. I can maybe do a few more depleting activities if I sandwich them in-between others that bring me joy and are revitalizing.

The hard choice for me comes when I am faced with the reality that it may be time to walk away from people and situations that are consistently depleting and filled with unnecessary drama. I used to feel guilty for saying no or avoiding certain people and situations. Today, I know in the process, I am saying yes to myself so I am better positioned to be of greater service in areas where I can make a difference.

As the Buddha is believed to have said, "If you cannot find a good companion to walk with, walk alone, like an elephant roaming the jungle. It is better to be alone than to be with those who will hinder your progress." Sometimes, I may need to let others go for a while or forever. I may feel deep grief and regret, but in the long run, my life is better off. It sometimes takes great faith, but I find when I close one door, other opportunities have been there waiting for me all along. After we reprioritize our life choices, we may realize it is time for more rejuvenation in our lives.

Rejuvenate

"Find joy in each day."

~ Saint Philip Neri

I scoffed when I first saw this quote. I thought this was frivolous and wasteful. Today, I realize I do my best work when I am feeling joy, when I am in the flow. Forcing hard work or long hours only gave me the false illusion of being useful and important. When in the flow of life's work, I am far more at ease, gentler, and so focused and on point that magic happens! I hope you find your joy and then hang out there most of your days. The world needs all of us doing our best work, in service, from our space of joy.

Activity: What brings you joy?

Take a moment and look back at your list of what you do on most workdays and on your days off. Add any more activities you do in a typical two-week period. Then, reflect on each activity and identify the ones that give you joy, a sense of renewal, a lightness of being. Which ones leave you feeling energized and rejuvenated? Just like it can be important to let go of depleting activities, it is equally, if not more important to our self-care and social change work to build in more times of joy and rejuvenation, especially when we are in stressful periods in our lives.

Activity: Remember why you started

Like jump-starting a car when it has run out of battery life, I find I feel re-energized when I take some time to get back in touch with my passion for this work. Take a moment to get quiet and centered, and then ask yourself: "Why did I start doing activism and change work?" Imagine that younger version of yourself, full of energy and vitality, believing change was possible. You may want to take the time to journal about your memories and reread them every few months when you may need an extra charge.

Find your source of passion

"You have to find what sparks a light in you so that you, in your own way, can illuminate the world."

~ Farnoosh Brock

In most every workshop I facilitate on creating inclusive organizations, I ask participants to reflect and talk about a source of their passion or commitment for creating greater equity and social justice in their organizations or society. After a few moments of sharing stories and passions, most people notice they feel much lighter and more energized. Passion is contagious. Connecting at a deep, authentic level with other change agents is motivating. Remembering why you started as well as some of the more current sources of your passion can be quick ways to rejuvenate yourself and others in the moment, especially when times are tough.

Acknowledge progress

One final way to balance the heaviness of all that is horrendous in the world and find more energy to keep going is to focus on and celebrate the small wins along the way. How often do you pause to acknowledge and identify progress, even though there is still a long way to go? It may be useful, for you individually or with groups of change agents, to regularly identify the shifts and changes that occur. Collect them up in writing or in pictures so you can keep a record along the way. Reviewing these signs of progress in times of despair might be just enough renewal to remind you that we have survived and made it through difficult times before. It is the everyday effort, the small successes along the way that pave the road to progress.

What brings you joy? When do you feel rejuvenated? Find out and do more of it!

Revolutionize

Once we have rested, refilled, reflected, reprioritized, and rejuvenated, it is now time to make meaningful changes in our lives to ensure we can stay in the work for the long haul. While we are working to revolutionize the world, we also need to revolutionize our lives. For me this meant and still means I have to be constantly vigilant and willing to shift how I choose to spend my time moment by moment. This may mean, as one workshop participant recently shared, "taking back control over my evenings and weekends so I only do the things I want to do and very few things I have to do." It may mean reallocating time you used to use eating at your desk to instead unplug from work for 30-minutes as you take a brisk walk with a colleague and only talk about inspiring topics. It may involve shifting how you exercise and listening to inspiring TEDx talks or podcasts as you release your stress on the treadmill.

A client shared how they revolutionized how they used their time after November 7, 2016:

"After the election, I have changed how much I consume social media. I barely use Facebook anymore and have switched to following only things that bring me joy or delight on Twitter. This way I am still connected, but not bogged down and depleted by the barrage of negativity and hopelessness."

I relate to her. I was feeling such despair and realized I needed to make some changes. I have switched from watching 1-2 hours of MSNBC each night to getting most of my news from emails from *The New York Times* and *The Washington Post*. I may still occasionally check in on TV to get a focused hit of thoughtful analysis, but I have cut out the endless inane opinion news and have felt a significant difference in my energy level.

> *"It doesn't matter how slowly you go as long as you do not stop."*
>
> ~ Confucius

Here is a clear recipe for failure for most people. Treat revolutionizing your life like a New Year's Resolution. How often have you made a long list of changes and commitments on December 31st, and then realized around late January that you had failed at them all? And then felt even worse about yourself in the process? It may be more effective to choose a few changes, maybe only 1 or 2, and focus on those until they have become a habit.

I was so excited the day they finally took off my cast until I saw how much my forearm had shrunk and how painful and stiff my wrist was. I used this wonderful Confucius bit of wisdom as a mantra as I slowly began stretching, exercising, and doing physical therapy to regain as much motion and strength as possible. In the past, I have berated myself and my body for how slowly it heals and have played on sprained ankles too early and re-injured them in the process. Rushing and urgency are not good self-care for me. Like a persistent turtle, I have slowly but surely done my exercises, patiently stretching the tight ligaments, and sending deep gratitude to my body for its healing processes.

Committing to a new, revolutionizing path to self-care is a huge step. It is then critical that we stay true to our plan and honor our new commitments to ourselves step by step, moment by moment, slowly and consistently moving along the trail to a more balanced life of sustainable activism and change work.

Community care

"I cannot sit and care for my body without being concerned with what happens to the bodies of my sisters. We are connected... it is our responsibility not as individuals, but as communities to create structures in which self-care changes to community care. In which we are cared-for and able to care for others.... We need to move the self-care conversation into community care. We need to move the conversation from individual to collective. From independent to interdependent."

~ Yashna Padamsee

We will not be able to sustain resistance and change efforts for the long haul if the seeming vast majority of change agents continue to view self-care as an individual act, not a community responsibility. When I finally started to take better care of myself, I was primarily focused on my own self-care, not on community self-care. I may have been useful as I led trainings about codependency, wellness, and self-care, but as I look back, I was only focused on helping individuals focus on themselves. I hadn't yet begun to understand how organizational climate, cultural values, and societal resources played a part in accessibility to self-care and community care.

> *"Spending time with people that I love and that unconditionally love me is my self-care. It is a way for me to practice the importance of community and of collective care that is integral to what makes it possible for me to live to fight another day."*
>
> ~ Alicia Garza

How often do you and your colleagues talk about self-care as a vital element of social change work? How often do you engage and interrogate the belief that self-care is selfish and a luxury only for the privileged? That self-care is a badge of dishonor, a sign you care more for yourself than for others? I believe part of our organizing work needs to involve our coming together in our communities for meaningful conversations about how we take care of each other and ourselves so we can sustain the work. As Angela Davis said, "Self-care has to be incorporated in all of our efforts. And this is something new. This holistic approach to organizing is, I think, what is going to eventually move us along the trajectory that may lead to some victories (Mirk, 2016)."

> *"The part can never be well unless the whole is well."*
>
> ~ Plato

If I had seen this quote a few decades ago, I would have had only one interpretation: The activist part of me cannot be healthy and useful unless my whole self is healthy and balanced. Today, I am beginning to see another message as well: Individuals cannot be healthy and effective change agents if there is not a primary focus on community care.

To create a collective approach to self-care, we may need to develop new ways to collaboratively share and support each other. How can change communities create a bartering system where people give what they can and get support to meet their needs as they share responsibilities for child care, offer massages to others, carpool, cook healthy meals for families, share produce from gardens and CSAs, integrate music, meditation, and yoga into community meetings, do errands for each other, and more? Mostly, it may be important to keep talking about the critical need to care for the welfare of each other in community in order to maintain the capacity to organize and facilitate meaningful change.

Take a moment and do a quick assessment of the other change agents in your life. How often do you check-in with them about their self-care? How often do you authentically share with them about how you are doing? Do you have colleagues and friends in this work who will notice and lovingly confront you if they are concerned you are close to burnout and passion fatigue? Who can help you strategize when you are getting run-down, running on empty?

As you reflect, you may notice you want more people in your community of self-care with whom you can honestly talk and strategize to create a more sustainable practice. You can start today by raising these issues and asking questions of some of the change agents and activists in your life. This may be one of the more important things we do in the short-term as we collectively find more ways to refuel and revitalize as individuals as well as create structures in community to sustain ourselves as we keep organizing, educating, and building the future we envision for generations to come.

Activity: What I intend to do differently

> *"The way you react has been repeated thousands of times, and it has become a routine for you. You are conditioned to be a certain way. And that is the challenge: to change your normal reactions, to change your routine, to take a risk and make different choices."*
>
> ~ Don Miguel Ruiz

I've been told it takes about 21-days of focused effort and practice to change old habits. The first step is to be deeply aware of our unproductive life choices and habits. The next step is to commit to consistent action to change our lives. It can be hard to get started. After I broke my wrist, I did not work out for many weeks. Once I decided it might be safe to get back on the elliptical, I found I had little motivation to get back into my routine. It had become a habit to not work out.

It may take extra energy, focus, and determination to push through this inertia and get started in a new way of living. While traveling last week, I worked out two days in a row, then came home and had two long walks over the next two days. I'm also lifting light weighs in-between writing sessions to get more energy and wake-up a bit more. Now that I have some traction and evidence that I am sleeping better from working out, I expect I can get back to my routine of working out 4-5 times a week.

How do you want your life to be different? And just as important, how willing are you today to make the necessary choices to manifest your intentions?

> *"We can't solve problems by using the same kind of*
> *thinking we used when we created them."*
>
> ~ Albert Einstein

Take a moment and review your previous answers on the worksheet, *How I Currently Spend My Time and Energy* www.drkathyobear.com/selfcare. Make some notes about what you are noticing and what ideas for change come to you. Next, look at your responses on the worksheet, *How Satisfied Are You?* and identify 3-5 areas of your life that you want to improve. Take a few deep breaths and imagine what your life would be like if these areas shifted towards greater balance, renewal, and regeneration? Use the worksheet, *What I Intend to Do Differently* www.drkathyobear.com/selfcare to make some notes about how you might feel differently and what else you might be able to do if you made changes in these areas of your life. Write down any ideas for possible new approaches: what you can add, let go of, or redesign in ways that improve your self-care and life balance. Finally, I recommend you share these initial thoughts and ideas with some people in your circle of family, friends, and change agents. Invite their feedback, advice, and support.

Once you have a few clear ideas for changes you are willing to make, make a commitment to yourself to start, tell others about your new efforts, and plan how you will reward yourself for your progress towards your goals. The more we make these changes in community and celebrate the small shifts and progress along the way, the greater chance we will succeed.

I may not have many answers or ideas for others. Our individual and collective self-care will look different for each person, each group. The old ways may not work anymore. What we used to do may not be enough anymore. On my own, there have been times I couldn't sustain a meaningful activist life. I have to believe that together, we can create new ways of being and engaging that are life fulfilling as we partner to dismantle oppressive systems all around us.

Just do it!

"Don't expect to see a change, if you don't make one."

~ John Assaraf

I haven't found any magic wands or shortcuts to changing my life. The way forward is simple, though not always easy. We have to just get started. Take one step, and then another.

I used to always wait to start something new until I knew how to do it, until I was sure I would succeed. What a prescription for failure! I wanted to do it perfectly or not at all. So, I waited until I knew enough, for the right time to begin, and most times, I never got started. I encourage my clients to try 1-2 new things each week and notice the impact, however small. I support them by setting up a system of accountability with me and/or someone in their daily life. We talk about their challenges of being a beginner, trying something new, and the frustration and awkwardness of not being competent when they are used to being the expert in so many ways.

Start today to make a difference in the rest of your life. You may never know the impact you will have as you show up as a far more effective change agent, for the long haul. I believe the tools and activities in this chapter can help you more effectively navigate external dynamics and create a more balanced, sustainable life as a social justice change agent. In the next chapter, I focus on self-care techniques that are more internal, that we need to do from the inside out.

CHAPTER 6
Creating More Self-Care From the Inside Out

"If you long for the world to be a saner, more loving place, please be advised that you must start inside. Care for your sick, anxious, exhausted self as lovingly as you want to care for every suffering thing."

~ Martha Beck

I bet you can relate to this client's story:

"I remember feeling so stressed out and counting the days until I could leave work on the four-day weekend away we had planned together. Everything was so perfect! Long walks together, afternoon naps, fabulous meals, and even a fun night out dancing. I felt so much more rested and relaxed as we drove back home. And after a good night's sleep, I felt ready to face my Monday back at work. People were excited to see me and interested in my weekend. The first couple of meetings went well and I felt like I was on a roll. Then Jake stopped into my office and told me about a major problem with our project and how we could easily miss our deadline if we didn't drop everything and pull all hands-on deck. All I could think was, 'What a disaster! How could I have let this happen? I never should have taken any time off! I should have done it all myself instead of delegating anything to him.' I literally could feel all my energy and enthusiasm from the weekend drain out of my body the longer he talked."

All too often, in my experience, we refill our energy stores and feel renewed excitement about work, and then at the first major difficulty we quickly lose any benefit from our time away. Like having a leaky tire, until you patch it up, you're not going very far. We end up feeling as exhausted as before our trip, but this time, we feel more resentment and anger, if not hopelessness that anything will ever change. We rarely notice the hole in our tire and are increasingly frustrated that nothing we try, weekends away, massages, or even regular exercise, seems to make any difference in the long run. The problem is we think the solution is more activity to release our stress when the answer may be to look within and focus on how to create greater self-care from the inside out.

Making different lifestyle choices is necessary, but not sufficient, to have enough energy and passion to sustain us as change agents. We have to be far more vigilant and intentional about what we put inside and nurture in our bodies, including our thoughts, beliefs, feelings, and intentions. We also need to be far more focused on what we need to release in order to show up as effective change agents for the long haul. In this chapter, I explore a wide variety of tools and strategies to create more self-care from the inside out.

Thought Work

*"Ships don't sink because of the water around them;
ships sink because of the water that gets in them.
Don't let what's happening around you get inside
you and weigh you down."*

~ Unknown Author

Our ships sink, we sink because of the thoughts we let in and the resulting emotions we feel. When I harbor unproductive thoughts and beliefs, I am far less effective as a change agent. I yearn for the time in my life when I will no longer link my sense of self-worth to the quality and quantity of my work in the world as well as when I will finally let go of any attachment to what people think of me. But if you are like me, we have so many negative, limiting thoughts that deplete our energy and decrease our capacity to create sustainable change. In this section, I take common negative thoughts we use to push ourselves into burnout and passion fatigue and offer suggested ways to shift them into more reasonable beliefs that can help us lead more balanced, productive lives as social justice change agents.

If I don't do it, it won't get done

I find great relief when I take the time to use Byron Katie's questions from *The Work* to analyze and shift my limiting, unproductive thoughts www.thework.com When I think, "If I don't do it, it won't get done," I can ask myself her key questions: "Is this true?" "How do I treat others and myself when I think this thought?" and "Who would I be if I didn't think this thought?" Using Byron Katie's tools to create "turn-arounds" is where I often get the quickest relief from the negative thought. My favorite is to find a thought that is the opposite of the one causing my stress. In this case, I can turn around the original thought to a new one, "If I don't do it, it will get done." At first, I usually shake my head at the absurdity of the new thought. However, if I stay with this process and work to find 3-5 examples from my life that prove this new thought is just as possible as the one causing me stress, then I begin to feel some relief.

Here are a few examples that helped me loosen my grip on the original stressful thought, "If I don't do it, it won't get done." There have been times when I didn't complete a task and someone else picked it up and actually did it in ways that better met the needs of the team. At another time, I was too sick to be on a planning call and a couple of younger staff members led the meeting, facilitated a great solution to the problem at hand, and got experience leading a project maybe sooner than I would have planned. As a result of how well it went, we shifted our meetings so I co-led each one with another staff member. Over time, I noticed an increase in engagement with more people taking initiative and offering creative ideas. Each of these situations helped me realize that sometimes the turn-around thought is true, "If I don't do it, it will get done." As a result, I might be far less controlling and stressed out and actually have less to do as more people take on additional responsibilities.

If I take time off, everything will fall apart.

Is it true? Have there been times in your life when you took time off, and nothing fell apart? And maybe things fell together in unexpected, positive ways? When I have taken time off to intentionally rest and recover, I came back to projects with far greater clarity and creativity. In addition, if I have effectively engaged others into covering for me while I am away, I may be surprised by the results.

I have to work extremely hard and put in long hours to create a quality product.

I grew up believing this thought and labored long and hard over many reports, training packets, and strategic plans. As I look back, I can easily find times when the opposite was true: "If I work extremely hard and put in long hours, I will create a lower quality product." I remember feeling deep anxiety about a strategic report I had to create. I probably worked 40-50 hours in relative isolation and produced a 75-page report, that as I look back, no one read or found useful. When I handed it in, the leader looked at it and asked for a 2-page executive summary. I was so discouraged and exhausted. Working harder and longer did not result in a useful result in this case. There are many other times I have worked smarter and developed very good products in short amounts of time. They may not have met my perfectionist standards, but they were far more than good enough for the needs in the moment.

The next time I think, I'm not working hard enough, I can ask myself: "Is this true?" And then I can consider alternative thoughts, such as: "If I work harder, I might not be working smarter;" "I get more done when I am well-rested and centered;" "I do better work when I am refreshed;" and, "It's usually better when I focus on quality over quantity."

I don't know enough. I should be learning more, reading more.

While I believe in lifelong learning as well as doing enough research to understand new dynamics or issues, I also know that I can never learn all there is to know about any given subject. I used to believe that I couldn't start anything new until I knew most everything about it and felt like an expert. Only lately have I realized I may never feel ready and prepared, that instead, I just may need to take a chance and leap. A colleague was hesitant to apply for the next level position, saying she wasn't ready. One of her mentors gently said, "You think I felt ready when I took that position? No, nor does anyone else. You learn on the job and bring all your wisdom and skills. You're as ready as you can be."

Instead of obsessing about how much I don't know and stressing myself out in the process, I can set a reasonable goal to do some research as I move into the project or experience and learn as I go. In my experience, if I ask lots of questions and engage others to use their insights and ideas, together we create what needs to happen.

I should be doing more.

Is that true? If you did more, would you be useful and healthy over time? Or would you be over-extended, easily triggered, and possibly get sick? When I am shoulding on myself, I find it useful to ask myself a few questions: "What is the root of my belief that

I should be doing more?" and, "What more do I think I could be doing?" Often, when I dig around for the roots behind my shoulds, I find another layer of deep grief and rage about the current dynamics in this country and the world. I feel powerless to make much of a difference. If I give myself the space to feel and release my emotions, I usually have more clarity to answer the second question about what else I could be doing. I easily identify a few more ways I can be useful. Instead of using guilt and shame to motivate myself, shoulding on myself, I can show up with more passion and effectiveness if I decide from a grounded place how I want to contribute and create greater change.

I can shift the original stressful thought, "I should be doing more" and focus on more productive thoughts, including: "If I over-exert myself I won't be of use to anybody;" and "I will check in with myself every day to see what more I can be doing, if anything." This powerful message from Howard Zinn has helped me stay grounded and focused on doing my part to create greater justice in the world:

"We don't have to engage in grand, heroic actions to participate in the process of change. Small acts, when multiplied by millions of people, can transform the world."

~ Howard Zinn

I have to be there for everyone. Be their everything.

I am hearing many more change agents feeling this way given the dire urgency of the seemingly unending crises and the continuing lack of resources and organizational support. When I am in high stress mode, I get far more tunnel vision. I tend to solve problems using tools that have worked in the past but don't take time to think creatively and outside the box I've created in my mind.

I may be pleasantly surprised if I take the time to ask, "Is it true?" If I share my concerns and feelings with a few colleagues and ask for their help identifying possible solutions, together we might find new solutions and resources I would have missed on my own. These thoughts help me loosen my attachment to this limiting belief. Instead, these revised statements help me be more centered and balanced: "If I keep trying to be everything for everyone, I eventually will get so burned out I won't be of any use at all"; "If I keep solving everyone's problems for them, they may never learn the skills or develop the resiliency to move through life without me"; and, "How can we build more capacity in the organization so there are more people who can support each other?"

Burnout is a sign you are doing great activist and change work.

Is it true? Is it possible that burnout is a sign that people don't know how to do activism very effectively? Is it possible that burned out change agents actually do more harm than good? Instead of wearing burnout and passion fatigue as badges of honor, what if we created movements where we focused on community care and celebrated effective strategies for change over face-time and exhaustion as evidence of commitment to the cause?

Self-care is selfish.

In a sense, it is. And could it still be a good thing and what we should want and need from all change agents? I imagine a world where all activists and change agents focus enough on their self-care that they show up energized, passionate, and clear thinking. Could it be the beliefs that self-care is only for the privileged and we have to work ourselves into exhaustion to create change actually help maintain the very oppressions we are trying to dismantle?

This is horrible. It shouldn't be happening.

I had these thoughts for quite a while after the 2016 election. I was feeling such shock, despair, and hopelessness. And I was not very useful to anyone. As long as I was railing against reality, I was stuck in this quagmire of rage and terror and took no meaningful action. I was reposting all sorts of articles and reactions on Facebook, and maybe that was helpful to others. But I wasn't helping to motivate, educate, or organize for change.

I shifted when I began to accept the reality of the current dynamics instead of focusing on what I believed should have happened. And while I wish with all my soul we were in very different circumstances, these revised thoughts help me stay on point and moving forward: Maybe this experience is preparing us for an even more significant leap forward toward greater justice for all; Maybe this is an important time to help millions more wake-up to the realities of the depth of oppression and violence we face and join the movements; and, Maybe there is something important I need to learn in these times so I can be even more effective in the future.

I don't know if any of these turn-around thoughts are truer than my original ones. What I do know is that I am far more centered and effective when I have shifted my limiting beliefs. I am a much more useful part of change efforts from this more grounded space.

When I am willing to accept what is and stay in the present moment, without futurizing or imagining the worst that could happen, I have far greater capacity to respond effectively and put my attention and energy into manifesting the world I envision.

Change is too slow. Nothing we've done has made any difference, so why bother?

I have had moments since the election when I wallowed and wondered if anything we had done really made any meaningful change in the world. Thoughts like these contribute to my staying stuck in despair and feeling powerless. If I shift my attention and focus instead on the wisdom of elders and those who have come before, to remember that social change work is not a sprint, but a marathon, then I can breathe more deeply as I prepare for the next leg of the journey. If I believe change should happen quickly and easily, at the first few set-backs or defeats I may feel so devastated that I may drop out feeling hopelessness. However, I can find the strength to stay in it if I listen to the wise counsel of change agents who have been working for liberation for decades. I heard their voices when I needed them most: "We have been here before;" and, "We have made it through harder, more difficult times and we will again if we stay true to our purpose and our vision." When I expect set-backs and reroutes in this marathon for change, I have far more resilience to persevere in the hard times and stay in it for the long haul.

Activity: Change your beliefs

I used to think these limiting beliefs were true no matter what. Like so many cultural messages I was socialized to believe without question, I am usually not as effective if I hold onto them without critical reflection.

Take a moment and write down some of the early messages you were taught about work, self-care, and creating change. As you review your list, is there one that you once believed to be true, but now view differently? For instance, I was taught that men are leaders of movements and women support them. Or maybe you once believed as I did that if you push too hard for changes, you will experience harsh consequences, maybe even be killed. Today, I believe people of all genders can lead change efforts as well as provide critical support, and while some people may experience dire punishment or death, most change agents do not.

Try to identify as many old beliefs that you no longer believe are true. Next, choose one thought or belief that you still hold onto that is undermining good self-care habits. For instance, "I have to be perfect;" "I can't make a mistake;" "People will be angry if I don't show up as much;" "I can't take a break;" or "I have to work 60-70 hours a week to get everything done."

Take a quiet moment to rewrite a few of these limiting, stressful thoughts using some of Byron Katie's tools in the earlier section. Ask yourself, "Is it true?" Create a turnaround by imagining the opposite of the statement and then look for evidence from your past or the lives of others that could support your revised statements being as true if not truer than the stressful one.

Release and let go: Do our inner healing work

Changing our limiting, unproductive thoughts is a critical step to creating greater self-care and resilience in our lives. It is necessary, but not sufficient. We must also continue to do our self-work to heal and release any other inner obstacles and barriers that block us from being the most magnificent, powerful change agents we can be.

> *"Where there's drama, there's unresolved trauma."*
>
> ~ Doreen Virtue

I know in my body what it feels like to have passion and focus on creating change. I also know what it feels like to get so worked up and angry about all that is horrible in the world that I am getting high off the adrenalin rush and usually far less effective in that state. I believed I was being useful, that I was an empowered part of an important movement, when in reality I was only spinning in my negative emotions, fighting against the system, and not taking productive action to create real change.

I started to become more useful when I shifted my focus from participating in all the drama and wasting my spirit fighting useless battles, to instead finding others who were passionate about working to build a more just society. Focusing on what we are against is exhausting and draining. Keeping our eyes on the prize of liberation and working day in and day out to create what is possible and what we envision gives me a source of energy and a sense of purpose that helps me through the hard times. As Les Brown said,

> *"Where your focus goes, your energy flows. Focus on what you want, where you are going, and what you are actively creating."*
>
> ~ Les Brown

Imagine what you are working to create. Hold that vision in your heart and your mind. Feel your emotions as you immerse yourself in the possibilities. Feel your passion as you know in your soul this is possible to manifest. We must dream individually and collectively about the future we are building as we use the motivation and energy we generate to bolster us as we face inevitable obstacles, barriers, and resistance.

How important is it?

Lately, I've realized I am not able to remember some things as crisply, like why I was mad about something a week ago or the reason I don't like somebody. When I remember how I will most likely forget or not care about some things over time, I find I have less attachment and resentment and don't take things as personally as I used to. I can pause and ask myself, "How important is it? Will this matter in a week, a month, or a year?" If I realize from my answers that this isn't worth getting upset over, then I have much more energy to focus on issues and events that truly matter.

Let go of rage

I used to believe that change agents needed to feel deep rage and anger to fuel their activism. As a result, I raged against the system and was deeply angry towards everyone who disagreed with me in order to be seen as a useful change agent. My past experiences of oppression and old unhealed traumas fueled my rage and kept me going. But I soon realized how carrying that intensity of rage depleted my energy, my health, and my soul. I came to believe I needed to heal, but was haunted by these fears: My identity is wrapped around my past experiences of oppression, who would I be if I healed? How can I be an effective change agent if I no longer have this depth of rage inside me? Will I lose all my passion and energy for the work? Will I drop out and disappear like so many other members of privileged groups? I swirled in these fears and irrational beliefs for far too long.

Today, I believe I can be a very effective, passionate change agent and not be fueled by the anger and pain from old, unresolved traumas. In fact, the more I have focused on my healing work and releasing old pain and rage, the greater clarity I have to be present in the moment and react to what is actually occurring, and not to retriggered memories or emotions from my past. You may find it helpful to read my book, *Turn the Tide: Rise Above Toxic Difficult Situations in the Workplace*, as you learn more tools and strategies to do your inner healing work to show up as more effective instruments of change.

I am grateful I have discovered new skills and approaches to manifest change and engage others that produce far better results than the ways I used to show up in unhealed, retriggered pain and rage. I want to be clear. I still feel deep anger and horror but I am responding to the realities in the moment, not clouded by my unresolved past.

Healing our past rarely happens overnight, in my experience. I have been on a long journey to identify, accept, experience, and release all the stuck emotions of my past. I needed to revise and shift many of the stories and beliefs I still held onto about old events. In the process, I have been able to rewrite unproductive stories and reclaim my history so I am no longer a victim of difficult, oppressive circumstances, but an empowered change agent creating my life.

Forgiveness

"Forgiveness is a process of giving up the old for something new. Old experiences and memories that we hold on to in anger, resentment, shame, or guilt cloud our spirit mind. The truth is, everything that has happened had to happen. It was a growth experience. There was something you needed to know or learn. If you stay angry, hurt, afraid, ashamed, or guilty, you miss the lesson. You will be stuck in a cloud of pain."

~ Iyanla Vanzant

I still struggle with forgiving, though I believe it is a critical part of healing and moving on. I hold onto the idea that if I forgive, I am condoning what someone did. I have wasted so much time, energy, and life force swirling in resentment, replaying stories over and over about how others did me wrong. To be fair, their behavior often was very unproductive and crossed a line, and yet I kept the dynamic alive by spinning my tale over and over and carrying around my ever-expanding anger and pain. Someone asked me once: "Do you want to be happy or right?" For so long I wanted to be right. If I was right, then it meant I would prevail someday, and until then I could be a martyr. Such misdirected energy. I weighed myself down with this anchor of anger and resentment. I was only hurting myself by clinging to the hurt and pain.

Sometimes, I still want to be right. And, I also now want to be happy, peaceful, and stress-free. Several times each day, I am faced with this choice: Do I want to be happy or right? When I choose happy, I often, over time, see a new way to engage others or be in the world that helps me resolve the situation over which I harbored such deep resentment. I benefit in many ways and so does everyone I encounter. When I forgive, I become free and release so much heaviness from my spirit.

I have come to realize that forgiveness doesn't mean forgetting and it doesn't mean coddling. I can forgive others and still hold them accountable for changing their behavior. I am more effective if I have forgiven them because I can now engage them out of care and passion rather than anger and resentment. I can be clear and compassionate as I give direct feedback and hold them accountable. When I don't, people rarely hear me anyway, much less change their behavior in my experience.

Commit to your healing journey

This may not be true for everyone, but I have noticed a pattern. It seems some, even many change agents, are attracted to social justice work because they share a history with the issue. One client talked about this connection between their passion and their commitment to the work:

"I spent two years as a first responder for a sexual assault program. I was passionate and dedicated to serving others but neglected to process and heal my own trauma of sexual abuse. I quit the position because I was moving, but I didn't get involved with any grassroots organizing or prevention programs for over a year. I had to learn how to balance my self-care and community care to have the resilience to be of service."

If we continue to avoid doing our own healing work, maybe even using our activism to distract us from it, we may come to a day when the pain from our past imprisons us as we are locked into unhealthy, unproductive patterns of behavior. We deserve supportive healing spaces to resolve old traumas and release our pent-up emotions so our past will let us go.

Release

"Darling, you feel heavy because you are too full of truth. Open your mouth more. Let the truth exist somewhere other than inside your body.

~ Della Hicks-Wilson

Can you imagine a community of care where change agents and activists easily and readily talk about all the ways they are healing their pasts so they can be more effective in the moment, the movement? I hope you find spaces for deep catharsis, loving emotional support, and inspirational feedback to guide you on your way. Whether you find healing spaces in 12-Step groups or Re-Evaluation Counseling communities, in therapy or religious counsel, through yoga or meditation, I hope you give yourself the gift of healing.

We are far better change agents when we heal our past. As one client commented:

"Recently, I have been focusing more on my healing work and staying connected to my mind and body. As a result, I have been able to dive deeper into my work as a social justice change agent. I have been more present, more authentic, and give more of myself because I have more to give."

In it for the long haul

I need to do my inner work and heal so I have the energy and resilience to stay in the process over time. This is a game of chess, not tic-tac-toe. We may not see many changes or much impact from some of our actions in our tenure in a specific organization or even in our lifetimes. But we need to know in our souls that every action we take is creating change and a part of a larger movement making a difference in the lives of hundreds of millions of people, maybe eventually billions.

Today, do what you do well, contribute from your zone of genius as you honor and appreciate those with skills and capacities that complement yours. Recognize small changes, the whispers of progress, and know what you do is a part of a far larger movement than bends toward justice.

And in these extremely challenging times, stay grounded in the belief that we are moving forward. To get out of bed in the morning, I have to believe that tens of thousands more people are waking up and getting involved in change efforts. I see them in my trainings, I see them on Facebook. With every horrendous new executive order or rollback of legislation, many more people are recognizing the urgency and dire need for them to do more and be more.

And we each must answer the call as well. The call to up our game, to work more effectively in groups and in coalitions with other organizations to continue to educate and raise awareness, organize resistance, get involved in leadership, and speak truth to power.

I hope you know and believe what you do makes a difference, and when you begin to forget, I hope you have many people around you or within a click or a call to remind you how you are one of many millions, and how all of our efforts are critical in this time of transformation and change.

I believe that what we are experiencing, all this hate and resistance, is actually the last gasp of oppression before significant transformational change breaks through. Believing this helps me find a deep source of passion and energy to keep going and to work in community, in partnership, to create the world we envision and know in our soul is possible.

When I am centered and grounded, I am far more useful than when I am exhausted and triggered all the time. Self-care matters. The choice is ours individually to make, but we live in a community that needs each and every one of us at our best as we continue to create greater liberation and justice for all. We need each other, we need to support each other in community self-care so we will have the resilience and passion to move ahead, one step at a time. Each step taking us closer to our vision.

Activity: What I intend to do differently from the inside out

"Don't be afraid to start over. It's a chance to build something better this time."

~ Unknown Author

Take a moment and reflect on your thoughts, beliefs, feelings, and intentions about social change work. Are there any areas you want to explore more? Are there thoughts and beliefs that may need shifting? Emotions that deserve releasing? Old wounds and issues that need healing? How will you give yourself the gift of healing so you can show up as a more effective agent of change? How will you recommit to your self-care and increasing community care so we all are in this together for the long haul?

CHAPTER 7
What Do I Do If...

We cannot do effective self-care in isolation or by ourselves. It might be easier if we could. Each day we have to negotiate to meet our individual needs with people in our personal lives as well as those within complex organizational structures. Maneuvering within our personal lives can be difficult enough, but trying to create meaningful work/life balance in community groups and organizations can seem impossible at times. The challenges of navigating through organizational cultures and climates often require us to use more advanced skills and strategies as we try to create systemic change that supports the well-being and self-care of all members of the organization. In this chapter, I explore some "What Do You Do If?" scenarios I commonly hear from clients and workshop participants and offer some tools and approaches that may be useful as you navigate complicated dynamics of self-care in your workplace and social justice organizations.

What should I do if...

What do I do if a few people of color are expected to do all the work?

A client shared a very common dynamic I hear in my consulting and training work:

"I have been so exhausted lately. I am working more late nights and coming in early just to have a quiet space to get some work done before all the meetings and phone calls. I know I've been more snappy with colleagues, but they don't step up enough. Me and the few other people of color on staff are doing all the heavy lifting with extra committees, task forces, and all the triage care we are giving to everyone in crisis with this new administration. All the while, our so-called white allies get to just focus on their regular job tasks. Their silence is violence."

I see this dynamic in most every organization I work with. Some teams have made some progress after having the space in a well-facilitated retreat to honestly talk about the impact of the current national dynamics on their lives at work, at home, and in the community and then explore the significant increase in demand for services and support that only a few staff of color are experiencing. The next question to confront is how to have more people, especially whites, actively engaged in the work. To move in this direction, it is critical that top leaders understand these dynamics and the negative impact on morale, productivity, and retention as they require that everyone in the organization develop the capacity to consistently show up to be an active partner in this work.

With clear leadership expectations, the next step might be to have an honest conversation among the team about their fears and concerns given the expected outcomes. Most likely, many whites will say they want to be more involved but are afraid they don't know enough, will be called racist if they make a mistake, and will let their colleagues of color down. With facilitated, engaged dialogue and problem-solving, some organizations have developed some of the key necessary structures for changing these organizational dynamics, including: increase the skill and competence of staff through training, white affinity work, and supervision; implement accountability processes that ensure consistent development and increased activity so everyone does their part; and regular meetings and retreats to assess progress and negotiate any further changes and solutions. My book, *But I'm NOT Racist: Tools for Well-Meaning Whites*, may provide some useful tools and approaches to facilitate this level of organizational change.

Unfortunately, many people I meet do not work in organizations with the required courage, leadership, and willingness to address these racist dynamics directly and make these significant organizational changes. For most staff of color in these situations, it may be useful to start by talking with their other colleagues of color to provide each other support, identify the common patterns of experience, and begin to strategize next steps as a group. In one organization, a group of colleagues identified a few whites on the team who they thought might be most receptive to changing their behaviors. They strategically decided who should approach each person and what they would recommend. As a result, a couple of whites realized the impact of their behaviors and committed to show up more by speaking up about issues of race in meetings, attending more programs to increase their visibility in the larger organization, talking with other white colleagues, and creating opportunities for all whites on the team to deepen their awareness and skills through affinity spaces and reading groups. The change was slow compared to what might have been possible with committed leadership, yet the staff of color felt some progress as they continued to meet and engaged the initial white colleagues in different ways. After a few months, some of the people of color noticed the direct impact of these changes as they experienced less stress and exhaustion in the work environment.

What do I do if I notice I am so stressed out, I'm beginning to lose motivation at work?

A workshop participant shared their experience:

"These past couple of weeks have been particularly overwhelming. I got so exhausted I began to lose motivation and was not a very good colleague or supervisor that week. As I isolated more, I felt alienated and disconnected from others, but wasn't sure how to remedy this."

Low motivation and isolation are common symptoms of burnout and passion fatigue. While not always easy or productive, it may be useful to start by talking with your supervisor to check-in about the impact of the most recent work dynamics. In this conversation, it would be important to talk about your commitment to the team and the organizational goals while also sharing how stressed and burned out you have been feeling lately. Be prepared to offer a few ideas for shifting the current dynamics, such as taking a day-off to focus on your self-care, working from home a day or two each month, delegating more, and talking to your team about what you are experiencing.

If you are feeling overwhelmed, my guess is many members of the team are as well. It can be useful to talk with the entire group about the overall level of stress, how they are feeling in this environment, and ideas for creating a more productive, balanced workplace. The team members might also appreciate your owning up to the negative impact of your recent triggered and stressed reactions as well as your commitment to focusing more on your self-care so you do not take your stress out on others.

If you find that you are not able to shift your behaviors on your own, you might consider exploring local options for support groups and individual coaching or therapy to give you the needed support to make life changes.

What if I already have a packed schedule and they keep giving me more to do?

A client shared how she sat down to try to negotiate with her supervisor:

"I was feeling nervous about the meeting, but knew I had to do something. After the normal pleasantries and asking about our weekends, I framed why I wanted to have this conversation, 'I've been feeling particularly stressed out and overwhelmed lately, and I'd like to talk through all that I am working on and see if you can help me prioritize more. I am finding I am working 10-12 hour days and on weekends to try to meet these deadlines, and I know if I keep this up, the quality of my work may be impacted. As you know, I want to do all I can to meet our goals and I'm hoping that talking this through with you may help me find some insights and ideas to juggle these responsibilities.'

As we talked, I was able to ask for more clarity on the actual deadlines on some projects which helped ease my immediate work load as well as explore alternative ways to get others involved in the process to share the responsibilities. I floated a couple of ideas that I thought could help me balance things more, including telecommuting a day every two weeks or so. This way I would save a couple hours of travel and actually get far more concentrated time to work on projects and reports. I was nervous about asking for my supervisor's advice, afraid they might think I couldn't hack it. I was pleasantly surprised by how willing they were to have me shift a few things off my plate and start working from home occasionally."

What if people think they own me?

So many clients have talked about the constant stress and impact on their personal life of always having to be available and on-call for any given crisis. Occasionally, yes, many jobs require that we immediately respond to an unexpected crisis. However, if crisis management has become the norm, this is not sustainable. It may be necessary to reassess and revise the structures, culture, and systems of the organization. A first step may be to talk with your supervisor about the pattern of your experience and the impact on you and your capacity to fulfill your overall job responsibilities. An idea might be to pull together a working group of the people who respond to crises and their direct supervisors to discuss the current dynamics and brainstorm possible solutions.

Many more university leaders are forming campus-wide intervention teams to not only become prepared to respond to crises, but to also recommend system-wide changes to minimize crises in the future. One outcome of this process is expanding the number of people who have increasing capacity to be the first-responders in challenging situations.

Another thought is to re-examine the cultural norms for those whose personal time is interrupted to manage an organizational crisis. Are they expected to show up for work the next day or is there a clear, stated policy that outlines the options to have a flexible schedule and/or work from home to rest and recover from the extra stress of being a first responder?

What if people keep scheduling over times I have blocked off for self-care?

If your team or organization has already had conversations about the need for work/life balance, then it might be easier to talk with the person who is scheduling over your time. I might start by asking for some of the background information that had them decide to schedule a meeting at that time. There may be a reasonable explanation for a one-time event. Most likely, this is a pattern and will need a different approach.

After understanding more about the specifics of one or more times they over-scheduled your calendar, I might say something like, "I see a dilemma that is impacting us both. You are being asked to find time for me to do certain things and I am committed to working out over lunch so I can get a renewed jolt of energy in the middle of the day so I can be most effective. I always plan to stay late to make up the time. What might be some ways we can work together to meet both of these needs?"

Hopefully, the scheduler may see a few options, including checking in with you each morning to clarify your schedule or sending you a text or email each time they want to schedule over your workout time so you can have a quick conversation to work something out.

If these interpersonal conversations do not yield the results you want, you may consider involving your supervisor in the process. If you are experiencing this dynamic, it may be an indicator of a larger organizational expectation that needs exploring and shifting. And possibly, the scheduler feels pressure from others at higher levels in the organization and may not have the positional power to feel they can say no.

What if I'm overwhelmed and it's faster to just do things myself?

At times, it can seem faster and easier to do something yourself than to take the time to explain a task, much less correct someone else's mistakes afterward. It may be true that you are the best person to do a task, and in addition, it may be true that another person may also be effective at it. They just may do it differently than you would. Part of the problem might be your expectations and shoulds about how something needs to be done or how ego-involved you are in being the only one who can do it right.

I have had to learn to let go on many levels and be open to new ways of doing things. I found it important to have a conversation with the person taking over a task to identify the vision and hoped for outcomes, the big picture. If we can agree on the end product and timeline, I can more easily let go of HOW things get done. I also need to accept that in the short-term, the person may need more supervision and direction, so it could take them longer to complete the task. However, this short-term investment of time and attention will most likely pay off in multiple organizational benefits, including the increased capacity of this person to do more as well as their resulting positive morale and self-esteem. As more people have greater capacity to take initiative and complete projects you used to coordinate, you may have more flexibility, time, and energy to work within your zone of genius.

If I don't do it, it won't get done.

This is a common belief related to the previous example. If there really is no creative way to get the task done that doesn't involve you burning out, then it may be useful to ask the questions, "So, what? What's the harm or cost if it doesn't get done on time or at all?" While these questions may seem horrifying to some, I am finding they help me better reprioritize to identify the more critical tasks as well as those that I might be able to put on the back burner for a while.

People keep springing urgent issues and tasks on me.

So, whose problem is this? I used to assume I had to do everything that someone said was urgent, no matter what was already on my schedule. Every time I said yes, I rewarded them for demanding I stop what I was doing to take care of their urgent matter. And as we know, what gets rewarded gets repeated.

While there may be some urgent situations we do need to address immediately, what if we occasionally try a different approach? We can start by asking a few questions: "Can you help me understand what you need and the timeframe you envision? How urgent is this and what would happen if it is not resolved in the next hour or two?" Sometimes, slowing down the process to explore these questions can help the person realize they are having a triggered reaction out of stress. Once they de-escalate their emotions a bit, you might be able to negotiate a more reasonable next step.

I encourage you to consider starting to say this more often when people demand you stop what you are doing to meet their needs: "Unfortunately, I can't help you on this right now. In the future, if you can give me more lead time, I can probably work something out." This response might prompt others to take more responsibility for their timing and find ways to better plan ahead. If we consistently stop what we are doing and jump to take care of other's needs, what are they learning in the process? What are we modeling for others in the workplace? And what is the cost to ourselves and our well-being?

What if everyone on the team is triggered and stressed out all the time?

One client told me how they dealt with these dynamics in this type of situation:

"Even though I regularly meet with direct reports and talk about workload and work/life balance as we review their roles and responsibilities, I was noticing a much higher level of stress, tension, conflict, and silly mistakes among the team members. I decided to use our next staff meeting to address these issues and talk more about our community of care. I ordered some snacks and had all sorts of fun toys on the table to play with as we ate and connected socially for the first part of the meeting. Some made fun objects out of clay as others did some finger painting.

To start the more formal part of our meeting, I asked this question: 'How is the painting you made like the stress we are feeling?' After getting a few responses, I continued, 'How is the clay object you made, like feeling stressed out?' People had a lot of fun and laughed as we made meaning in these ways. This was a great way to break the ice to then talk about how people were feeling lately and the level of stress on the team.

As we moved along, I asked for specific situations that were stressful and needed our collective attention. As several people talked about how hard it was to concentrate given the noise level in the office, we came up with an innovative idea to try: We designated one of the meeting rooms as a "creative space" a few hours each day so individuals or small groups of people can have a quiet space to focus more on key projects. We then talked about other ideas that could help us as individuals and collectively better navigate this increased time of stress as well as others in the future.

As we moved to closing out the meeting, I reiterated my commitment to creating a productive work environment where people feel motivated to work hard and be creative, but not over-stressed and burned out. I encouraged team members to talk with me personally or bring issues up during team meetings if they start to notice or feel a rise in tension and conflict again. Things seemed better in the office over the next week or two and several people thanked me for the meeting."

When you try to focus more on self-care, and someone says, "You're being selfish!"

A white client shared how they struggle to find work/life balance:

"As a white person, I struggle finding a balance between self-care and times I slip into white privilege. Am I trying to avoid the work because it feels too hard like when I am getting confronted on my racist attitudes and behaviors? For those of us with privileged identities, doing social justice work requires us to lose some of the comfort and ease so we can disrupt and change the system that is set up for our needs and comfort. Yet at the same time, if I don't take care of myself, I show up in ways that negatively impact others and undermine our efforts. When I am not my best self, I often show up in ways that perpetuate the very oppressions I am committed to dismantling.

So many clients and workshop participants with one or more privileged groups, especially white people, express deep concern over focusing on their well-being. They say they don't believe they deserve self-care and are worried about what people in marginalized groups will think about them if they do take time for life balance. I appreciate their awareness of the societal inequities and how oppression disproportionately impacts one's ability to access both time and resources for self-care. Yet, if we do not take good care of ourselves, we react unproductively out of stress and tension much of the time. As a result, we show up in ways that severely undermine and damage efforts to create greater inclusion and social justice in our organizations and in society.

My guess is the person who may call you selfish is also in dire need of self-care themselves. Instead of shrinking back in a flight or freeze stress reaction, can you imagine responding with comments such as: "I sometimes do worry I am being selfish. Yet, I believe we all deserve far more self-care and well-being in our lives. Is there a way I can support you and everyone else in our group to talk about what we need and find ways to support our collective self-care? I believe we may do better work if we find ways to center our well-being while we also focus on achieving our goals."

I feel overwhelmed by how much I am NOT doing

One reason we may feel overwhelmed and procrastinate is we are trying to do a number of tasks that are not our strength. One participant realized, as an introvert, she was really good at organizing and writing, which are critical, yet hard to find, skills for creating change. While these may not be the most recognized or rewarded contributions, she made peace with focusing on how she could best contribute while she let others do what they were good at which included the marching and protesting.

It might be important to help group members work within their zones of genius. Can you imagine having a group or team conversation where everyone gives positive feedback and appreciation for each other's contributions and talents? The next step is to openly explore new ways to maximize how each person can share their strengths and possibly reallocate tasks to those whose skills might be a better fit.

What We Could Do If...

Imagine how your work environment would be different if you had more conversations at all levels in the organization about ways to shift the culture, climate, and daily practices to support the self-care and work/life balance of each member of the team. I believe you would unleash greater creativity, productivity, and customer care as people felt more valued, respected, and supported to bring their full selves to the workplace. Instead of trying to survive and get by in a toxic workaholic environment, people would have more freedom to thrive and contribute their talents and capacities for the greater good of the people they serve.

CHAPTER 8
Conclusion

I answered an unexpected call late afternoon on a Friday from a client who was in deep pain and anguish over failing to deliver on a very critical training session, or at least that was how she was making meaning in the moment. I just listened as she told me the story through tears and deep pain. After about five minutes, she began to talk more slowly and with less intense emotions. I asked her to take three very deep breaths and to notice her physical surroundings as she felt her body sitting in her chair. When I sensed she was a bit more grounded, I asked a few questions to get a clearer view of the details and found out that 1) a few people had given critical feedback on the evaluations, 2) many more people had come up to thank her for the session and express their gratitude for the experience, and 3) she was deeply exhausted from all the planning and preparation. I definitely related to her experience and shared a story of a recent workshop and how I obsessed about the 2-3 negative comments in the evaluations for days while over-looking how many people had noted how powerful and meaning-ful the training had been for them. I then told her how I respected how she had reached out for support, given how in the past, I had isolated in my shame and guilt after sessions when I thought I had failed as a facilitator.

We talked further about the specifics of the group dynamics and she said she felt much better after debriefing with me. I then decided to explore issues of self-care more directly. I asked her how she was intending to take care of herself for the next few days. Together we developed a plan for deep self-care, including: eating a healthy meal for dinner, taking a hot bath, and getting a solid night's sleep. For the next day, she thought taking a long walk with friends followed by a nap sounded lovely. I added a few thoughts including to drink lots of water, listen to inspiring music, take another nap on Sunday, and arrange for a massage. By then she was laughing a bit and seemed to have more perspective on the whole situation.

On our call early that next week, we explored in greater depth the various steps and actions she had taken leading up to the train-ing. I asked her to walk me through the past few weeks of planning and we soon realized a few choices that may have contributed to her feeling so exhausted and deeply triggered. She had worked late most nights for the past week to try to finish the design and train-ing materials. As a result, she had felt depleted as she began the workshop. In addition, she noticed how she hadn't been working out and had been eating more fast food and drinking more caf-feine in order to get everything done on time.

We then started to explore some of her expectations and limiting beliefs that may have helped create this perfect storm. She realized she had expected the session to go perfectly as planned and had hoped to receive mostly outstanding evaluations. She hadn't expected as much resistance from participants and so was unprepared for the backlash and negative criticism. It had felt personal, as opposed to a predictable outcome from people who were new to issues of equity and social justice.

In subsequent sessions, we explored and started to heal some of the intrapersonal roots and dynamics that fueled her triggered response, including attachment to being liked and approved of; needing to be perfect and seen as fully competent; and some internalized sexism she still struggled with. I could relate to each and every one of these and hoped she felt supported as I shared similar stories about my own journey.

Self-care involves so many aspects of our lives. When we are in the middle of a stressful period, it is hard to pull back and notice what we are doing in the moment. It is often only on reflection that we can see the patterns and actions that resulted in our needing far more self-care than we were bringing into our lives. We need to listen to the whispers each and every day, or we will end up, once again, in difficult struggles and in dire need of a more intense self-care intervention.

When I broke my wrist in the airport rushing to make my flight, I knew it was time for me to take stock of things. I had been moving so fast those months since the election, doing too much, and not paying attention or taking care of myself. I hope I will finally learn this lesson this time.

"Everything in life comes to you as a teacher.
Pay attention. Learn quickly."

~ Cherokee Saying

I hope my story and those of so many others in this book will help you pay attention and stop ignoring the gentle whispers and nudges in your life, messages that you need to change. I hope you decide to take a closer look at your life and make some different choices, before it is too late.

The costs of burnout and passion fatigue can be emotionally, physically, and spiritually debilitating. We are at our best as change agents when we are rested and rejuvenated. Our stressed out, triggered reactions often have a negative impact on those we love and care about and often undermine our values and social justice goals. As many have written and spoken about more recently, these current dynamics of oppression and terror may demand that we develop new ways of organizing and creating liberation. Central to these changes may be our increased capacity to sustain ourselves and our communities for the long haul through intentional, persistent self-care and community care.

These horrific times can seem overwhelming, yet I am inspired seeing so many people feeling the call to step up to do more, to be more. But if we are reacting out of deep terror and urgency, we are rarely effective. We have seen similar times and we have persevered and made progress, and we will again. What is needed is not frantic, erratic activity, but thoughtful, strategic organizing designed to create sustainable change. I will not be very useful if I am exhausted, fueled by deep fear, and spinning in anxiety. We each have an ethical responsibility to create space for self-care and community care as well as space for our healing work so we show up as effective change agents in all that we do.

I have taken far too long to learn these lessons. I wonder how much more effective and impactful my life would have been if I had created more balance and self-care these past decades. Instead of stopping out, dropping out, or showing up in an exhausted, triggered haze, I wonder what difference I could have made as a consistent, powerful, steady voice for social justice.

We are at a crossroads. We can stay exhausted in our passion fatigue and burnout, making a small difference with our lives or we can choose the path of transformation and self-care. The choice is yours. I hope you choose to live in greater balance each and every day for the rest of your life, to stay in it for the long haul.

Further Reading

Brown, B. *3 Ways to Recharge When You're Burned Out.* http://www.oprah.com/inspiration/brene-brown-how-to-handle-burnout#ixzz4dVkHRjon

Coles, R. (1994). *The Call of Service: The Witness to Idealism.* Mariner Press.

Gorski, P. (2015). *Relieving Burnout and the "Martyr Syndrome" Among Social Justice Education Activists: The Implications and Effects of Mindfulness,* Urban Review 47: 696-716.

Hooks, B. (2003). Teaching Community: A Pedagogy of Hope. Routledge.

Jones, K. & Okun, T. (2001). White supremacy culture. http://www.cwsworkshop.org/PARC_site_B/dr-culture.html

Katie, B. *The Work.* http://thework.com

Korn, G. (2015). *Laverne Cox gives us life advice.* https://www.nylon.com/articles/life-advice-laverne-cox

Lorde, A. (1988). A Burst of Light. Fireband.

Mirk, S. (2016). *Audre Lorde thought of self-care as an 'act of political warfare.* https://www.bitchmedia.org/article/audre-lorde-thought-self-care-act-political-warfare

Obear, K. H. (2017). But I'm NOT Racist: Tools for Well-Meaning Whites. Difference Press.

Obear, K. H. (2016). Turn the Tide: Rise Above Toxic, Difficult Situations in the Workplace. Difference Press.

O'Hara, M. E. (2017). *#NotMyPresident's Day: Endless Protests Raise the Specter of 'Resistance Fatigue'.* http://www.nbcnews.com/news/us-news/notmypresident-s-day-endless-protests-raise-specter-resistance-fatigue-n722351

Pesta, A. (2008). *Michelle Obama Keeps It Real.* http://www.marieclaire.com/politics/news/a2132/michelle-obama-interview-media/

Piepzna-Samarasinha, L. L. (2012). *for badass disability justice, working-class and poor lead models of sustainable hustling for liberation.* http://www.brownstargirl.org/blog/for-badass-disability-justice-working-class-and-poor-lead-models-of-sustainable-hustling-for-liberation

Pozner, J. L. (2016). *Self-Care in the Multiracial Movement for Black Lives.*

http://www.colorlines.com/articles/self-care-multiracial-movement-black-lives

Roisin, F. (2015). *Self-Care And Survival: An Interview With Janet Mock.* https://thehairpin.com/self-care-and-survival-an-interview-with-janet-mock-6fba0fed0e5a

Smiley. T. (2009). Doing What's Right. Anchor.

Acknowledgments

I would not be here but for all the generosity, wisdom, and patience of amazing mentors and colleagues who have helped me and supported me on my journey as a social justice change agent. To the faculty in the Social Justice Education Program at The University of Massachusetts, Amherst, I am deeply grateful for all I learned with you. To my colleagues at Elsie Y. Cross Associates, I carry so many of the lessons and insights with me as I do my work every day.

To Rev. Dr. Jamie Washington, thank you for our journey to greater self-care, healing, and wholeness. I learn from you each time I am blessed to be with you.

I am indebted to all the workshop participants, clients, and survey participants who so freely shared their stories and life experiences with me. Thank you for all the immeasurable wisdom and examples you gave me.

I am deeply grateful to all the amazing and powerful healers who have helped me learn, grow, heal, and change over the years, especially Verena, Candi, Lisa, and Amy.

To T.J. Jourian, thank you for your wonderful research to find such powerful quotes for the book.

To Angela Lauria, Cynthia Kane, and the other incredible people at The Difference Press. Your support, insights, and expert editing have been invaluable. Thank you for helping me birth this book.

To the Morgan James Publishing team: Special thanks to David Hancock, CEO & Founder for believing in me and my message. To my Author Relations Manager, Gayle West, thanks for making the process seamless and easy. Many more thanks to everyone else, but especially Jim Howard, Bethany Marshall, and Nickcole Watkins.

To my loving wife and life partner, Paulette Dalpes. Thank you for all your amazing support and love on this journey. I learned so many of these lessons through walking our path together. I would not have been able to share the breadth of this work without all the ways I have grown with you.

To all the social justice change agents, past, present and future—thank you for your powerful work, your deep investment and commitment to change, and your unending passion to create the world we envision and know in our soul is possible. We may not see the full manifestation of peace and social justice in our life-times, but I know each and every action we take moves up closer to our vision. Together we can and together we will.

About the Author

Kathy Obear, Ed. D., is a social justice change agent who works with leaders and members of organizations to create greater equity and inclusion in every aspect of their lives. Several times in her career, she almost dropped out of social change work due to the depth of burnout and passion fatigue she experienced. Kathy pulls from over 30 years of experience as a trainer, consultant, speaker, and coach to help change agents deepen their capacity, confidence, and courage to manifest meaningful, sustainable organizational change. Her work supports those experiencing passion fatigue and burnout to reignite their energy and recommit to creating true liberation and justice for all.

If you want to know how to accelerate your capacity to create transformative change in the world, contact her at:

www.drkathyobear.com/contact

Kathy lives in Colorado with her wife and two amazing kitty muses who helped her write this book!

Website: www.drkathyobear.com

Email: Kathy@drkathyobear.com

Thank You

Thank you for reading my book! I hope you found a sense of connection and community as well as inspiration to continue on your journey to create greater self-care, community care, and social justice in the world.

To show my appreciation, I want to give you access to my recent self-assessment, ***How Much Do You Need Self-Care? A Checklist for Change Agents.*** I hope this tool supports your continued development and commitment to create meaningful, sustainable change.

Visit www.drkathyobear.com/selfcare to access this resource and others to support your healing journey.

For information about **working with me to deepen your capacity to ignite meaningful, sustainable change in the world,** visit my website, www.drkathyobear.com or **contact me** directly www.drkathyobear.com/contact.

Morgan James
Speakers Group

www.TheMorganJamesSpeakersGroup.com

We connect Morgan James published authors with live and online events and audiences who will benefit from their expertise.

Printed in the USA
CPSIA information can be obtained
at www.ICGtesting.com
JSHW021508020424
60423JS00005B/146